EXECUTIVE

ORDERS

Going Around Congress
To Make the President's

𝕷𝖆𝖜𝖘 𝖔𝖋 𝖙𝖍𝖊 𝕷𝖆𝖓𝖉

A Very Scary Nonfiction Book

By David Lawrence

Of Dundalk

EXECUTIVE ORDERS

The President's Laws of His Choosing

FOREWORD

You have seen the President in pictures with his feet up on the Oval Office desk.

You have seen the President on TV with his magic marker saying that with a pen he can authorize any law he pleases!

In just under eight years (as of June 30, 2016), he has signed 244 executive orders into law.

In this book, the first eight chapters list each executive order law consecutively followed by the exact wording of the Declaration of Independence and the U.S. Constitution with all 27 amendments.

You are invited to join my blog to vent your opinions and read other's comments.
http://www.dlawrenceexecutiveaction.wordpress.com

In the last chapter A Very Scary Time, I give my comments on specific "Laws of the President's Land."

Attention Active Military and Veterans, did you know the President has signed five executive orders totaling 173 pages of his Laws making changes to the Manual of Military Courts Martial! WATCH OUT you may have violated his new Laws!

TABLE OF CONTENTS
EXECUTIVE ORDERS 2009-JUNE 2016

ACKNOWLEDGMENTS

First of all, I would like to thank the World Wide Internet and all its Search Engines. Without it, research would take longer and slow down fact checking.

Second thanks to the North Point Public Library in Dundalk, Maryland. Where you can spend days or weeks reading history, or anything else that has ever been published in book form, free. Most of this information comes from United States websites available to any member of the general public who owns a personal computer and takes the time to do the research. I did, and I love you Mr. or Mrs. Internet.

Also, much credit must go to the Federal Register and The Daily Journal of The United States Government in Washington, D.C. Many Thanks!

INTRODUCTION

To the readers, the contents of Executive Orders is not a political statement on behalf of any party or candidate. This book is intended for three purposes only.

1) To inform the American public about presidential executive orders and how to access them at any time during a president's term.

2) The copy of the Declaration of Independence and the Bill of Rights are intended as a permanent reference source.

3) If in fact you are experiencing a disagreement on the wording of either of the two documents, the reader will have a copy to right any wrong iteration that may occur.

FREE SPEECH: In my research of college and high school textbooks on history, students are taught the right establishment answers. Whose right answers; history's or the current establishments? Students are taught to read and answer as written and printed in the current textbooks.

We put that question to young adults in community and state colleges and received the same answers repeatedly. In order to get a passing grade you must answer the way the textbook tells you to or you WILL receive a failing grade. This means that whatever the textbook says you will carry that answer all of your life. (After all, printed books are always correct...) YOU WILL follow the dog's wagging tail.

Tell the same lie repeatedly and people will soon believe "IT MUST BE TRUE." - Adolph Hitler. 1932

In all of my surveys, I received the same response "I read the answer in a book." Well, now I want the true answer and response "guaranteed" by the first Amendment to the United States Constitution.

In this book, you will read actual United States history as written by the framers of our democracy in plain English and readable type.

No words will be changed. Ask your grandparents if you can't understand certain words or terms. No comments or conclusions will be added. Your own ability to read and understand will be your only guide. Forget, for the purposes of this book, all texts that guide you to THEIR conclusions.

Your challenge is to read an executive order from the United States president and match it up against the United States Constitution or one of its amendments.

Go to my blog site with a pro or con on at least two of the executive orders that effect American life as you see it. Include a scorecard of minus 1 to 10 (or plus) 1 to 10 on all the executive orders that effect everyday life.

It is said that the president writes his own laws of the land with a pen. Is this even legal? You decide by matching it with the Constitution of the United States of America.

The second book of this series will contain some of your responses. So, like on social media, what you put out there will stay in print for all to read forever.

Be true to yourself when answering as you might influence politics of the future when presidents and other elected officials see the will of the American voters. E-mails that have hate, racial, or religious tones will be deleted so don't waste your time on that.

Attacks on me personally for assembling this book are most welcome and will make a fine chapter to the next book in this series.

Guarantee and disclaimer: I give my solemn word that no comment made in writing will bring forth any legal actions against persons or entities who respond.

Permission is hereby granted to copy, reprint, and discuss or quote any part of this book, cover to cover.

The first amendment to the constitution applies as our esteem founders first committed it to parchment paper plainly, to be read and understood by all Americans and I fully understand and support the right of FREE SPEECH.

Nothing in this book is meant to be politically correct. (PC) Certain buzzwords or phrases are meant to hide the true meaning of a situation and give me cause to think bad words and develop a headache. Below are some of my favorites...

1. Political correct
2. At the end of the day
3. The right thing to do
4. Turn the other cheek
5. Turn a blind eye
6. Be nice to them and they will be nice to you

7. Crap runs downhill (seen it ooze in all directions)
8. Strike while the iron is hot (excuse me)
9. It's for the children
10. Either for or against me

Each of my ten could be a chapter or a whole book of jokes on the comic hour. Email yours to my blog so we can compile a more lasting buzzword list for the next book in this series.

Send me at least ten of your buzzwords to show how much the public responds. Let's hear some real feeling behind them...

The President of the United States took office at noon on January 20, 2009 and started issuing executive orders on January 20, 2009 for a current total of two hundred forty-four orders as of June 30, 2016.

The executive orders are listed by year, their number, the full description or title, and are noted if the order revokes a previous president's order. As you read the executive orders, space is provided for you to make notes.

The web site to go to and read all the pages of the complete executive order that catches your interest is as follows:

www.federalregister.gov/executive-orders/Barack-Obama/2016

It's interesting, that as you read through the Executive orders, you will find over 40 of them have to deal about Appointing Advisors, committees, boards and various councils.

The President of the United States appears to nominate each one, without congressional approval in most cases. Is this a slick way to give out jobs to friends or large donors...don't know if it is, but the thought is. Very, very interesting. Yes/No! Let me know.

The executive orders are listed by Year starting with 2016 and going back to 2009. Any executive orders issued after June 30 2016 will be listed on my blog for reference. Please visit my blog for discussion.

http://www.dlawrenceexecutiveaction.wordpress.com

Chapter 1: In the year 2016

In the first half year of 2016, the President published sixteen executive orders from EO 13716 through EO 13731.

EO 13731: global entrepreneurship: Three pages. Signed 24 June 2016: Published 29 June 2016.

Notes:

EO 13730: 2016 amendments to the manual for courts-martial, United States 28 pages. Signed 20 May 2016: Published 26 May 2016.

Notes:

EO 13729: a comprehensive approach to atrocity prevention and response: Five pages. Signed 18 May 2016: Published 23 May 2016.

Notes:

EO 13728: Wild land-Urban interface federal risk mitigation: five pages, signed 18 May 2016: Published 20 May 2016.

Notes:

EO 13727: facilitation of a presidential transition: Three pages, signed 6 May 2016: Published 11 May 2016

EO 13726: blocking property and suspending entry into the United States of persons contributing to the situation in Libya: four pages, signed 19 April 2016: Published 21 April 2016.

Notes:

EO 13725: steps to increase competition and better inform consumers and workers to support continued growth of the American economy: Three pages, signed 15 April 2016: Published 20 April 2016.

Notes:

EO 13724: amending executive order 12137: 1 page, signed 9 April 2016: Published 13 April 2016.

Notes:

EO 13723: establishing the inherent resolve medal: two pages, signed 30 March 2016: Published 1 April 2016.

Notes:

EO 13722: blocking the property of the government of North Korea and the workers party of Korea and prohibiting certain transactions with respect to North Korea: six pages, signed 15 March 2016: Published 18 March 2016.

Notes:

EO 13721:   developing an integrated global engagement center to support government-wide counterterrorism communications directed abroad and revoking executive order 13584: Four pages, signed 14 March 2016: Published 17 March 2016.

Notes:

EO 13720:   delegation of certain authorities and assignment of certain functions under the trade preferences extension act of 2015: 4 pages, signed 2 February 2016: Published 2 March 2016.

Notes:

EO 13719:   establishment of the federal privacy council, 5 pages, signed, 9 February 2016: Published 12 February 2016.

Notes:

EO 13718: Commission on enhancing national cyber security: Four pages, signed 9 February 2016: Published 12 February 2016.

Notes:

EO 13717: establishing a Federal earthquake risk management standard: Six pages, signed 2 February 2016: Published 5 February 2016.

Notes:

EO 13716: revocation of executive orders 13574, 13590, 13622, and 13645 with respect to Iran, amendment of executive order 13628 with respect to Iran, and provision of implementation authorities for aspects of certain statuary sanctions outside the scope of U.S. Commitments under the joint comprehensive plan of action: Six pages, signed 16 January 2016: Published 21 January 2016.

Notes:

Chapter 2: In the year 2015

In 2015, the President Published 29 executive orders, from EO 13687 through EO 13715.

EO 13715: adjustments of certain rates of pay: 14 Pages, signed 18 December 2015: Published 23 December 2015.

Notes:

EO 13714: strengthening the senior executive service: Seven pages, signed 15 December 2015: Published 18 December 2015.

Notes:

EO 13713: Half day closing of executive departments and agencies of the federal government on Thursday 24 December 2015: 2 pages, signed 11 December 2015: Published 16 December 2015.

Notes:

EO 13712: blocking property of certain persons contributing to the situation in Burundi: Four pages, signed 22 November 2015: Published 25 November 2015.

Notes:

EO 13711: establishing an emergency board to investigate disputes between New Jersey transit rail and certain of its employees represented by certain labor organizations: Five pages, signed 12 November 2015: Published 17 November 2015.

Notes:

EO 13710: termination of emergency with respect to the actions and policies of former Liberian president Charles Taylor: four pages, signed 12 November 2015: Published 16 November 2015.

Notes:

EO 13709: National security metal: Two pages, signed 2 October 2015: Published 7 October 2015.

Notes:

EO 13708: continuance or reestablishment of certain federal advisory committees: Three pages, signed 30 September 2015: Published 5 October 2015.

Notes:

EO 13707: using behavioral science insights to better serve the American people: Three pages, signed 15 September 2015: Published 18 September 2015.

Notes:

EO 13706: establishing paid sick leave for federal contractors: Four pages, signed 7 September 2015: Published 10 September 2015.

Notes:

EO 13705: designating the international renewable energy agency as a public international organization entitled to enjoy certain privileges, exemptions, and immunities: four pages, signed 3 September 2015: Published 9 September 2015.

Notes:

EO 13704: presidential innovation fellows program: Five pages, signed 17 August 2015: Published 20 August 2015.

Notes:

EO 13703: implementing the national HIV AIDS strategy for the United States for 2015-2020: Four pages, signed 30 July 2015: Published 4 August 2015.

Notes:

EO 13702: creating a national strategic computing initiative: Four pages, signed 29 July 2015: Published 3 August 2015.

Notes:

EO 13701: delegation of certain authorities and assignment of certain functions under the bipartisan congressional trade priorities and accountability act of 2015. Five pages, signed 17 July 2015: Published 23 July 2015.

Notes:

EO 13700: establishing an emergency board to investigate disputes between New Jersey transit rail and certain of its employees represented by certain labor organizations: Three pages, signed 15 July 2015: Published 20 July 2015.

Notes:

EO 13699: establishing the advisory board on toxic substances and worker health: Two pages, signed 26 June 2015: Published 01 July 2015.

Notes:

EO 13698: hostage recovery activities: Six pages, signed 24 June 2015: Published 29 June 2015.

Notes:

EO 13697:   amendment to executive order 11155, Awards for special capability in career and technical education: Three pages, signed 22 June 2015: Published 25 June 2015: amends EO 11155 of 23 May 1964.

Notes:

EO 13696: 2015 amendment to the manual for courts–martial, United States: 48 pages, signed 17 June 2015: Published 22 June 2015:   ref: EO 11473 of 13 April 1984.

Notes:

EO 13695: termination of emergency with respect to the risk of nuclear proliferation created by the accumulation of a large volume of weapons-usable fissile material in the territory of the Russian federation: One page, signed 26 May 2015:   Published 28 May 2015: revoked EO 13617 of 25 June 2012.

Notes:

EO 13694: blocking the property of certain persons engaging in significant malicious cyber- enabled activities: Three pages, signed 01 April 2015: Published 02 April 2015.

Notes:

EO 13693: planning for federal sustainability in the next decade: 16 pages: signed, 19 March 2015: Published 25 March 2015: Amends: EO 13327 of 4 February 2004: EO 13432 of 14 May 2007.

Notes:

EO 13653 of 1 November 2013: EO 13677 of 23 September 2014: Revokes: EO 13423 of 24 January 2007: EO 13514 of 5 October 2009: memorandum of 24 May 2011: memorandum of 2 December 2011: memorandum of 21 February 2012: memorandum of 5 December 2013.

Notes:

EO 13692: blocking property and suspending entry of certain persons contributing to the situation in Venezuela: Five pages, signed 8 March 2015: Published 11 March 2015.

Notes:

EO 13691: promoting private sector cyber security information sharing: Seven pages, signed 13 February 2015: Published 20 February 2015: amends: EO 12829 of 6 January 1993: See EO 13549 of 18 August 2010.

Notes:

EO 13690: establishing a federal flood risk management standards and a process for further soliciting and considering shareholder input: four pages, signed 30 January 2015: Published 4 February 2015.

Notes:

EO 13689: enhancing coordination of national efforts in the arctic: six pages: signed 21 January 2015: Published 26 January 2015.

Notes:

EO 13688: Federal support for local law enforcement equipment acquisition: Three pages, signed 16 January 2015: Published 22 January 2015.

Notes:

EO 13687: imposing additional sanctions with respect to North Korea: Five pages, signed 2 January 2015: Published 6 January 2015: See EO 13466 of 26 June 2008: EO 13551 of 30 august 2010: EO 13570 of 18 April 2011.

Notes:

Chapter 3: In the year 2014

In 2014 the president Published 31 executive orders from EO 13656 through EO 13686.

Notes:

EO 13686: adjustments of certain rates of pay: 12 pages, signed 19 December 2014: Published 24 December 2014: supersedes EO 13655 of 23 December 2013.

Notes:

EO 13685: blocking property of certain persons and prohibiting certain transactions with respect to Crimea region of Ukraine: Three pages, signed 19 December 2014: Published 24 December 2014: See: EO 13660 of 6 March 2014.

Notes:

EO 13661 of 16 March 2014: EO 13662 of 20 March 2014.

Notes:

EO 13684: establishment of the president's task force on 21st century policy: Two pages, signed 18 December 2014: Published 23 December 2014.

Notes:

EO 13683: amendments to executive orders 11030, 13653, 13673: 4 pages, signed 11 December 2014: Published 16 December 2014: amends: EO 11030 of 19 June 1962.

Notes:

EO 13653 of 1 November 2013: EO 13673 of 31 July 2014:   see: EO 13653 of 1 November 2013.

Notes:

EO 13682:   closing of executive departments and agencies of the federal government on Friday 26 December 2014: 4 pages, signed 5 December 2014: Published 10 December 2014.

Notes:

EO 13681:   improving the security of consumer financial transactions: Five pages, signed 17 October 2014: Published 23 October 2014.

Notes:

EO 13680: ordering the selected reserve and certain individual ready reserve members of the Armed Forces to active duty: One page, signed 16 October 2014: Published 23 October 2014.

Notes:

EO 13679: establishing an emergency board to investigate a dispute between the south Eastern Pennsylvania transportation authority and its locomotive engineers represented by the brotherhood of locomotive engineers and trainmen: Two pages, signed 10 October 2014: Published 17 October 2014.

Notes:

EO 13678: conversion authority for criminal investigations (special agents) of the bureau of alcohol, tobacco, firearms and explosives: Two pages, signed 3 October 2014: Published 8 October 2014.

Notes:

EO 13677: climate-resilient international development: Eight pages, signed 23 September 2014: Published 26 September 2014: amended by EO 13693 of 19 March 2015.

Notes:

EO 13676: combating antibiotic-resistant bacteria: Five pages, signed 18 September 2014: Published 23 September 2014.

Notes:

EO 13675: establishing the president's advisory council on doing business in Africa: Five pages, signed 5 August 2015: Published 8 August 2015.

Notes:

EO 13674: revised list of quarantineable communicable diseases: One page, signed 31 July 2014: Published 6 August 2014.

Notes:

EO 13673: Fair pay and safe workplaces: Seven pages, signed 31 July 2014: Published 5 August 2014: See EO 11246 of 24 September 1965: EO 13658 of 12 February 2014: EO 13683 of 11 December 2014.

Notes:

EO 13672: further amendments to executive order 11478, equal employment opportunity in the federal government, and executive order 11246, equal employment opportunity: Two pages, signed 21 July 2014: Published 23 July 2014: Amends: EO 11246 of 24 September 1965: EO 11478 of 8 August 1969.

Notes:

EO 13671: taking additional steps to address the national emergency with respect to the conflict in the Democratic Republic of the Congo: Five pages, signed 8 July 2014: Published 10 July 2014: amends EO 13413 of 27 October 2006.

Notes:

EO 13670: establishing an emergency board to investigate disputes between the South Eastern Pennsylvania transportation authority and certain of its employees represented by certain labor organizations: Three pages, signed 14 June 2014: Published 18 June 2014.

Notes:

EO 13669: 2014 amendments to the manual for courts-martial, United States: 29 pages, signed 13 June 2014: Published 18 June 2014: amends EO 12473 of 13 April 1984.
Notes:

EO 13668: ending immunities granted to the development fund for Iraq and certain other Iraqi property and interests in property pursuant to EO 13303, as amended: See EO 13303 of 22 May 2003: EO 13364 of 29 November 2004: EO 13315 of 28 August 2003.

Notes:

EO 13667: blocking property of certain persons contributing to the conflict in the Central African Republic: Seven pages, signed 12 May 2014: Published 15 May 2014.

Notes:

EO 13666: expanding eligibility for the defense meritorious service medal: One page, signed 18 April 2014: Published 23 April 2014.

Notes:

EO 13665: non-retaliation for disclosure of compensation information: Two pages, signed 8 April 2014: Published 11 April 2014.

Notes:

EO 13664: blocking property of certain persons with respect to South Sudan: Five pages, signed 3 April 2014: Published 7 April 2014.

Notes:

EO 13663: Establishing an emergency board to investigate disputes between Long Island Railroad Company and certain of its employees represented by certain labor organizations: Five pages, signed 20 March 2014: Published 25 March 2014: see EO 13654 of 21 Nov. 2013.

Notes:

EO 13662: blocking property of additional persons contributing to the situation in Ukraine: Five pages, signed 20 March 2014: Published 24 March 2014: See EO 13660 of 6 March 2014: EO 13661 of 16 March 2014: EO 13685 of 19 December 2014.

Notes:

EO 13661: blocking property of additional persons contributing to the situation in Ukraine: Six pages, signed 16 March 2014: Published 19 March 2014: See: EO 13660 of 6 March 2014: EO 13662 of 20 March 2014: EO 13685 of 19 December 2014.
Notes:

EO 13660: blocking property of certain persons contributing to the situation in Ukraine: Five pages, signed 6 March 2014: Published 10 March 2014: See: EO 13661 of 16 March 2014: EO 13662 of 20 March 2014: EO 13685 of 19 December 2014.

Notes:

EO 13659: streamlining the export/import process for America's business: Six pages, signed 19 February 2014: Published 25 February 2014.

Notes:

EO 13658: establishing a minimum wage for contractors: Six pages, signed 12 February 2014: Published 20 February 2014: see EO 13673 of 31 July 2014.

Notes:

EO 13657: changing the name of the national security staff to the national security council staff: One page, signed 10 February 2014: Published 14 February 2014.

Notes:

EO 13656: establishment of Afghanistan and Pakistan strategic partnership office and amendment to executive order 12163: 4 pages, signed 17 January 2014: Published 24 January 2014: amends EO 12163 of 29 September 1979.

Notes:

Chapter 4: In the year 2013

In 2013 the president Published 21 executive orders EO 13635 through EO 13655.

EO 13655: adjustments of certain rates of pay: 12 pages, signed 23 December 2013: Published 31 December 2013: supersedes: EO 13641 of 5 April 13: EO 13686 of December 2014.

Notes:

EO 13654: establishing an emergency board to Investigate disputes between the Long Island Railroad Company and certain of its employees represented by certain labor organizations: Three pages,   signed 21 November 2013:   Published 26 November 2013: See: EO 13663 of 20 March 2014.

Notes:

EO 13653: preparing the United States for the impacts of climate change: Eight pages, signed 1 November

2013: Published 6 November 2013: amended by EO 13693 of 19 March 2015: See: EO 13677 of 23 September 2014: EO 13683 of 11 December 2014.

Notes:

EO 13652: continuance of certain federal advisory committees: Four pages, signed 30 September 2013: Published 4 October 2013: Amends: EO 13043 of 16 April 1997: EO 13231 of 16 October 2001: EO 13515 of 14 October 2009: EO 13538 of 19 April 2010: EO 13600 of 9 February 2012: plus supersedes many other executive orders.

Notes:

EO 13651: prohibiting certain imports of Burmese jadeite and rubies: Four pages, signed 6 August 2013: Published 9 August 2013.

Notes:

EO 13650: improving chemical facility safety and security: Five pages, signed 1 August 2013: Published 7 August 2013.

Notes.

EO 13649: accelerating improvements in HIV prevention and care in the United States through the HIV care continuum initiative: five pages, signed 15 July 2013: Published 18 July 2013: See: EO 13703 of 30 July 2015.

Notes:

EO 13648: combating wildlife trafficking: five pages, signed 1 July 2013: Published 5 July 2013.

Notes:

EO 13647: establishing the White House Council on Native American affairs: Four pages, signed 26 June 2013: Published 1 July 2013:

Notes:

EO 13646: Establishing the president's advisory council on financial capability for young Americans: Five pages, signed 25 June 2013: Published 28 June 2013.

Notes:

EO 13645: authorizing the implementation of certain sanctions set forth in the Iran freedom and counter-proliferation act of 2012 and additional sanctions with respect to Iran: Nine pages, signed 3 June 2013: Published 5 June 2013.

Notes:

EO 13644: amendments to executive order 13639: 1 page, signed 21 May 2013: Published 24 May 2013

Notes:

EO 13643: 2013 amendments to the manual for courts- martial, United States: 52 pages, signed 15 May 2013: Published 21 May 2013.

Notes:

EO 13642: making open and machine readable the new default for government information: Three pages, signed 9 May 2013: Published 14 May 2013.

Notes:

EO 13641: adjustments of certain rates of pay: 12 pages, signed 5 April 2013: Published 11 April 2013:

supersedes: EO 13635 of 27 December 2012: EO 13655 of 23 December 2013.

Notes:

EO 13640: continuance of advisory council: One page, signed 5 April 2013: Published 10 April 2013: Continued by: EO 13652 of 30 September 2013.

Notes:

EO 13639: establishment of the presidential commission on election administration: Two pages, signed 28 March 2013: Published 3 April 2013:

Notes:

EO 13638: amendments to executive order 12777: 4 pages, signed 15 March 2013: Published 21 March 2013.
Notes:

EO 13637: Administration of reformed export controls: Six pages, signed 8 March 2013: Published 13 March 2013.

Notes:

EO 13636: improving critical infrastructure cyber security: Eight pages, signed 12 February 2013: Published 19 February 2013: See: EO 13549 of 18 August 2010: EO 12866 of 30 September 1993: EO 13563 of 18 January 2011: EO 13609 of 1 May 2012: EO 13610 of 10 May 2012

Notes:

EO 13635: adjustments of certain rates of pay: 12 pages, signed 27 December 2012: Published 3 January 2013: Supersedes: EO 13594 of 19 December 2011: superseded by EO 13641 of 5 April 2013:
Notes:

Chapter 5: In the year 2012

In 2012 the president Published 38 executive orders from EO 13597 through 13634.

EO 13634: reestablishment of advisory commission: Three pages, signed 21 December 2012: Published 31 December 2012: continued by: EO 13652 of 30 September 2013: See: EO 13555 of 19 October 2010.

Notes:

EO 13633: closing of executive departments and agencies of the federal government on Monday, December 24, 2012: 2 pages, signed 21 December 2012: Published 28 December 2012.

Notes:

EO 13632: establishing the Hurricane Sandy rebuilding task force: Four pages, signed 7 December 2012: Published 14 December 2012.

Notes:

EO 13631: reestablishment of advisory group: Three pages, signed 7 December 2012: Published 12 December 2012: continued by: EO 13652 of 30 September 2013:

EO 13630: establishment of an inter-agency task force on commercial advocacy: Three pages, signed 6 December 2012: Published 11 December 2012: See EO 13534 of 11 March 2010.

Notes:

EO 13629: establishing The White House homeland security partnership council: Five pages, signed 26 October 2012: Published 2 November 2012.

Notes:

EO 13628: authorizing implementation of certain sanctions set forth in the Iran threat reduction and Syrian human rights act of 2012 and additional sanctions with respect to Iran: Seven pages, signed 9

October 2012: Published 12 October 2012: amends: EO 13622 of 30 July 2012.

Notes:

EO 13627: strengthening protections against trafficking in persons in federal contracts: Five pages, signed 25 September 2012: Published 2 October 2012.

Notes:

EO 13626: gulf coast ecosystem restoration: Four pages, signed 10 September 2012: Published 13 September 2012: see: EO 12777 of 18 October 1991: EO 13554 of 5 October 2010.

Notes:

EO 13625: improving access to mental health services for veterans, service members, and military families: Four pages, signed 31 August 2012: Published 5 September 2012.

Notes:

EO 13624: accelerating investment in industrial energy efficiency: Five pages, signed 30 August 2012: Published 5 September 2012:

Notes:

EO 13623: preventing and responding to violence against women and girls globally: signed 10 August 2012: Published 16 August 2012.

Notes:

EO 13622: authorizing additional sanctions with respect to Iran: Six pages, signed 30 July 2012: Published 2 August 2012: amended by: EO 13628 of 9 October 2012: See: EO 12957 of 15 March 1995: EO 13628 of 9 October 2012.

Notes:

EO 13621: White House initiative on educational excellence for African-Americans: Six pages, signed 26 July 2012: Published 1 August 2012: continued by: EO 13652 of 30 September 2013: See: EO 13532 of February 2010.

Notes:

EO 13620: taking additional steps to address the national emergency with respect to Somalia: Five pages, signed 20 July 2012: Published 24 July 2012: see: EO 13536 of 12 April 2010.

Notes:

EO 13619: blocking property of persons threatening the peace, security, or stability of Burma: Three pages, signed 11 July 2012: Published 13 July 2012: amends: EO 13448 of 18 October 2007: EO 13464 of 30 April 2008.

Notes:

EO 13618: assignment of national security and emergency preparedness communications functions: five pages, signed 6 July 2012: Published 11 July 2012: Revokes: EO 12472 of 3 April 1984: amends: EO 12382 of 13 September 1982: See: EO 12333 of 4 December 1981: EO 13526 of 29 December 2009.

Notes:

EO 13617: blocking property of the government of the Russian federation relating to the disposition of highly enriched uranium extracted from nuclear weapons: 5 pages, signed 25 June 2012: Published 27 June 2012: See : EO 12938 of 14 November 1994: EO 13085 of

26 May 1998: EO 13159 of 21 June 2000: revoked by EO 13695 of 26 May 2015.

Notes:

EO 13616:   accelerating broadband infrastructure deployment: Four pages, signed 14 June 2012: Published 20 June 2012: see: EO 13604 of 2 March 2012.

Notes:

EO 13615: providing an order of succession within the office of management and budget: Two pages, signed 21 May 2012: Published 24 May 2012: revokes: EO 13261 of 13 January 2005.

Notes:

EO 13614: providing an order of succession within the environmental protection agency: Two pages, signed 21 May 2012: Published 24 May 2012: revokes: EO 13261 of 19 March 2002 EO 13344 of 7 July 2004.

Notes:

EO 13613: providing an order of succession within the department of commerce: Two pages, signed 21 May 2012: Published 24 May 2012: Revokes EO 13242 of 18 December 2001.

Notes:

EO 13612: providing an order of succession within the department of agriculture: Two pages, signed 21 May 2012: Published 24 May 2012: Revokes EO 13542 of 13 May 2010.

Notes:

EO 13611: blocking property of persons threatening the peace, security, or stability of Yemen: Three pages, signed 16 May 2012: Published 18 May 2012.

Notes:

EO 13610: identifying and reducing regulatory burdens: Four pages, signed 10 May 2012: Published 14 May 2012: see: EO 12866 of 30 September 1993: EO 13563 of 18 January 2011: EO 13707 of 15 January 2015.

Notes:

EO 13609: promoting international regulatory cooperation: Three pages, signed 1 May 2012: Published 4 May 2012: see: EO 12866 of 30 September 1993: EO 13563 of 18 January 2011.

Notes:

EO 13608: prohibiting certain transactions with and suspending entry into the United States of foreign sanctions evaders with respect to Iran and Syria: 5 pages, signed 1 May 2012: Published 3 May 2012: see: EO 12938 of 4 November 1994: EO 12957 of 15 March 1995: EO 13224 of 23 September 2001: EO 13338 of 1 May 2004.

Notes:

EO 13607: establishing principles of excellence for educational institutions serving service members, veterans, spouses, and other family members: Four pages, signed 27 April 2012: Published 2 May 2012.

Notes:

EO 13606: blocking The property and suspending entry into the United States of certain persons with respect to grave human rights abuses by the governments of Iran and Syria via information technology: 6 pages, signed 22 April 2012: Published 24 April 2012: See: EO 12957 of 15 March 1995: EO 13338 of 11 May 2004.

Notes:

EO 13605:   supporting safe and responsible development of unconventional domestic national gas resources: Four pages, signed 13 April 2012: Published 17 April 2012.

Notes:

EO 13604: improving performance of federal permitting and review of infrastructure projects: Six pages, signed 22 March 2012: Published 28 March 2012: See: EO 13563 of 18 January 2011: EO 13580 of 12 July 2011: EO 13616 of 14 June 2012.

Notes:

EO 13603: National defense resources preparedness: 10 pages, signed 16 May 2012 Published 22 May 2012: see EO 11858 of 7 May 1975: EO 12472 of 3 April 1984: EO 12656 of 18 November 1988.

Notes:

EO 13602: establishing a White House Council on strong cities, strong communities: four pages, signed 15 March 2012: Published 20 March 2012.

Notes:

EO 13601: establishment of the interagency trade enforcement center: Three pages, signed 28 February 2012: Published 5 March 2012.

Notes:

EO 13600: establishing the president's global development council: Five pages, signed 9 February 2012: Published 14 February 2012: Amended: EO 13652 of 30 September 2013: continued by: EO 13652 of 30 September 2013.

Notes:

EO 13599: blocking property of the government of Iran and Iranian financial institutions: Six pages, signed 5 February 2012: Published 8 February 2012: See: EO 12957 of 15 March 1995: EO 12170 of 14 November 1979: EO 12281 of 19 January 1981: EO 12628 of 9 October 2012.

Notes:

EO 13598: assignment of functions relating to certain promotion and appointment actions in the Armed Forces: Four pages, signed 27 January 2012: Published 2 February 2012.

Notes:

EO 13597: establishing visa and foreign visitor processing goals and The task force on travel and competitiveness: Three pages, signed 19 January 2012: Published 24 January 2012.

Notes:

Chapter 6: In the year 2011

In 2011 the president Published 34 executive orders from EO 13563 through 13596.

EO 13596: amendments to executive orders 12131 and 13539: 2 pages, signed 19 December 2011: Published 27 December 2011: Amends: EO 12131 of 4 May 1979: EO 13539 of 21 April 2010.

Notes:

EO 13595: instituting a national action plan on women, peace, and security: Three pages, signed 19 December 2011: Published 23 December 2011.

Notes:

EO 13594: adjustments of certain rates of pay: 13 pages, signed 19 December 2011: Published 23 December 2011: supersedes: EO 13561 of 22 December 2010.

Notes:

EO 13593: 2011 amendments to the manual for courts-martial, United States: 15 pages, signed 13 December 2011: Published 16 December 2011.

Notes:

EO 13592: improving American Indian and Alaskan native education opportunities and strengthening tribal colleges and universities: Five pages, signed 2 December 2011: Published 8 December 2011: Revokes: EO 13270 of 3 July 2002: EO 13336 of 30 April 2004: EO 13585 of 30 September 2011.

Notes:

EO 13591: continuance of certain federal advisory committees: 4 pages, signed 23 November 2011: Published 30 November 2011: see: EO 13521 of 24 November 2009: EO 13522 of 9 December 2009: EO 13532 of 26 February 2010: EO 13538 of 22 April 2010: EO 13539 of 21 April 2011: EO 13540 of 26 April 2010: EO 13549 of 18 August 2010: EO 13544 of 10 June 2010: EO 13631 of 7 December 2012.

Notes:

EO 13590:   authorizing the Imposition of certain sanctions with respect to the provision of goods, services, technology, or support for Iran's Energy and petrochemical sectors: Four pages, signed 20 November 2011: Published 23 November 2011: See: EO 12957 of 15 March 1995.

Notes:

EO 13589: promoting efficient spending: Four pages, signed 9 November 2011: Published 15 November 2011:   see: EO 13576 of 13 June 2011.
Notes:

EO 13588: reducing prescription drug shortages: Two pages, signed 31 October 2011:   Published 3 November 2011.

Notes:

EO 13587: structural reforms to improve the security of classified networks and a responsible sharing and safeguarding of classified information: Five pages, signed 7 October 11: Published 13 October 11.

Notes:

EO 13586: establishing an emergency board to investigate disputes between certain railroads represented by the national carriers conference committee of the national Railway labor conference And their employees represented by certain labor organizations: three pages, signed 6 October 2011: Published 12 October 2011.
Notes:

EO 13585: continuance of certain federal advisory committees: Two pages, signed 30 September 2011: Published 7 October 2011: supersedes EO 13511 of 20 September 2009: Superseded in part by: EO 13652 of

30 September 2013: Amends: EO 13515 of 14 October 2009.

Notes:

EO 13584: developing an integrated strategic counterterrorism Communications initiative and establishing a temporary organization to support certain government wide communications activities directed abroad: Three pages, signed 9 September 2011: Published 15 September 2011.

Notes:

EO 13583: establishing a coordinated government-wide initiative to promote diversity and inclusion in The federal workforce: Five pages, signed 18 August 2011: Published 23 August 2011: See: EO 13078 of 13 March 1998: EO 13163 of 26 July 2000: EO 13171 of 12 October 2000: EO 13518 of 9 November 2009: EO 13548 of 26 July 2010.

Notes:

EO 13582:   blocking property of the Government of Syria and prohibiting certain transactions with respect to Syria: Three pages, signed 17 August 2011: Published 22 August 2011: See: EO 13338 of 11 May 2004: EO 13399 of 25 April 2006: EO 13460 of 13 February 2008: EO 13572 of 29 April 2011: EO 13573 of 18 May 2011.

Notes:

EO 13581:   blocking property of transnational criminal organizations: Three pages, signed 24 July 2011: Published 27 July 2011.

Notes:

EO 13580:   interagency working group on coordination of domestic energy development and permitting in

Alaska: Five pages, signed 12 July 2011: Published 15 July 2011: See EO 13547 of 19 June 2010.

Notes:

EO 13579: regulation and independent regulatory agencies: Four pages, signed 11 July 2011: Published 14 July 2011: See: EO 12866 of 30 September 1993: EO 13565 of 18 January 2011.

Notes:

EO 13578: coordinating policies on automotive communities and workers: Two pages, signed 6 July 2011: Published 11 July 2011: revokes: EO 13509 of 23 June 2009.

Notes:

EO 13577: establishment of the select USA initiative: Three pages, signed 15 June 2011: Published 20 June 2011.

Notes:

EO 13576: delivering an efficient, effective, and accountable government: Five pages, signed 13 June 2011: Published 16 June 2011.

Notes:

EO 13575: establishment of the White House rural council: Five pages, signed 9 June 2011: Published 14 June 2011.

Notes:

EO 13574: Authorizing the implementation of certain sanctions set forth in the Iran sanctions act of 1996, as amended: Three pages, signed 23 May 2011:

Published 25 May 2011: See: EO 12957 of 15 March 1995.

Notes:

EO 13573: blocking property of senior officials of the government of Syria: Four pages, signed 18 May 2011: Published 20 May 2011: see: 13338 of 11 May 2004: EO 13399 of 25 April 2006: EO 13460 of 13 February 2008: EO 13572 of 29 April 2011: EO 13582 of 17 August 2011.

Notes:

EO 13572: blocking property of certain persons with respect to human rights abuses in Syria: three pages, signed 29 April 2011: Published 3 May 2011 see: EO 13338 of 11 May 2004: EO 13399 of 25 April 2006: EO 13460 of 13 February 2008: EO 13573 of 18 May 2011: EO 13582 of 17 August 2011.

Notes:

EO 13571: streamlining service delivery and improving customer service: Three pages, signed 27 April 2011: Published 2 May 2011: see: EO 12862 of 11 September 1993.

Notes:

EO 13570: prohibiting certain transactions with respect to North Korea: Four pages, signed 18 April 2011: Published 20 April 2011: see: EO 13466 of 26 June 2008: EO 13551 of 30 August 2010: EO 13687 of 2 January 2015.

Notes:

EO 13569: amendments to executive orders 12824, 12835, 12859, and 13532, reestablishment pursuant to EO 13498, and revocation of EO 13507: 4 pages, signed 5 April 2011: Published 8 April 2011: Amends: EO 12824 of 7 December 1992: EO 12835 of 25 January 1993: EO 12859 of 16 August 1993: EO 13532 of 26 February 2010: Revokes: EO 13507 of 8 April 2009: see: EO 13498 of 5 February 2009.

Notes:

EO 13568: extending provisions of the international organizations immunities act to the office of the high representative in Bosnia and Herzegovina and the international civilian office in Kosovo: Three pages, signed 8 March 2011: Published 11 March 2011.

Notes:

EO 13567: periodic review of individuals detained at Guantánamo Bay Naval Station pursuant to the authorization for use of military force: seven pages, signed 7 March 2011: Published 10 March 2011: see: EO 13491 of 22 January 2009: EO 13492 of 22 January 2009.

Notes:

EO 13566: blocking property and prohibiting certain transactions related to Libya: Four pages, signed 25 February 2011: Published 2 March 2011.

Notes:

EO 13565: Establishment of the intellectual property enforcement advisory committees: Three pages, signed 8 February 2011: Published 11 February 2011.

Notes:

EO 13564: establishment of the president's Council on jobs and competitiveness: Two pages, signed 31 January 2011: Published 3 February 2011: Revokes: EO 13501 of 6 February 2009.

Notes:

EO 13563: improving regulation and regulatory review: Three pages, signed 18 January 2011: Published 21 January 2011: see: 12866 of 30 September 1993: EO 13579 of 11 July 2011: EO 13604 of 22 March 2012: EO 13609 of 1 May 2012: EO 13610 of 10 May 2012: EO 13636 of 12 February 2013: EO 13707 of 15 September 2015:

Notes:

Chapter 7: In the year 2010

In 2010 the president Published 37 executive orders from EO 13526 through EO 13562:

EO 13562: recruiting and hiring students and recent Graduates: Seven pages, signed 27 December 2010: Published 30 December 2010: Supersedes: EO 12015 of 26 October 1977:
Revokes: EO 13318 of 21 November 2003: EO 13162 of 6 July 2000: EO 13561: (NOT LISTED ON FILE)

Notes:

EO 13560: White House Council for community solutions: Two pages, signed 14 December 2010: Published 17 December 2010.

Notes:

EO 13559: fundamental principles and policy making criteria for partnerships with Faith based and other neighborhood organizations; Seven pages, signed 17 November 2010: Published 22 November 2010: amends: EO 13279 of 12 December 2002: see: EO 13198 of 29 January 2001: EO 13199 of 29 January 2001: EO 13498 of 5 February 2009.

Notes:

EO 13558: export enforcement coordination center: Two pages, signed 9 November 2010: Published 15 November 2010.

Notes:

EO 13557: providing an order of succession within the department of justice: Two pages, signed 4 November 2010: Published 9 November 2010: 2 pages, signed 4 November 2010: Published 9 November 2010: revokes: EO 13481 of 9 December 2008.

Notes:

EO 13556: controlled unclassified information: Three pages, signed 4 November 2010: Published 9 November 2010: revokes: memorandum of 7 May 2008: See: EO 13526 of 29 December 2009.

Notes:

EO 13555: White House initiative on educational excellence for Hispanics: Seven pages, signed 19 October 2010: Published 22 October 2010: See: EO 13634 of 21 December 2012: EO 13652 of 30 September 2013.

Notes:

EO 13554: establishing the golf coast ecosystem restoration task force: Five pages, signed 5 October 2010: Published 8 October 2010: see: EO 13626 of 10 September 2012.

Notes:

EO 13553: blocking property of certain persons with respect to serious human rights abuses by the government of Iran and taking certain other actions: Five pages, signed 9 September 2010: Published 1 October 2010: see: EO 12957 of 15 March 1995.

Notes:

EO 13552: (No title available) Ten pages, signed 31 August 2010: Published 3 September 2010: See: EO 12473 of 13 April 1984.

Notes:

EO 13551: blocking property of certain persons with respect to North Korea: Three pages, signed 30 August 2010: Published 1 September 2010: see: EO 13466 of 26 June 2008: EO 13570 of 18 April 2011: EO 13687 of 2 January 2015:

Notes:

EO 13550: establishment of Pakistan and Afghanistan support office: Two pages, signed 18 August 2010: Published 23 August 2010.

Notes:

EO 13549: classified national security information program for state, local, tribal, and private sector entities: Six pages, signed 18 August 2010: Published 23 August 2010: See: EO 12333 of 4 December 1981: EO 12829 of 6 January 1993: EO 12068 of 2 August 1995.

Notes:

EO 13548: increasing federal employment of individuals with disabilities: Three pages, signed 26 July 2010: Published 30 July 2010: see: EO 13163 of 26 July 2000: EO 13583 of 18 August 2011.

Notes:

EO 13547: stewardship of the ocean, our coasts, and the Great Lakes: Seven pages, signed 19 July 2010: Published 22 July 2010: revokes: EO 13366 of 17 December 2004.

Notes:

EO 13546: optimizing the security of biological select agents and toxins in the United States: Six pages, signed 2 July 2010: Published 8 July 2010.

Notes:

EO 13545: president's council on fitness, sports, and nutrition: Five pages, signed 22 June 2010: Published 28 June 2010: see: EO 10830 of 24 July 1959.

Notes:

EO 13544: establishing the National prevention, health promotion, and public health Council: Four pages, signed 10 June 2010: Published 16 June 2010: see: EO 13591 of 23 November 2011: EO 13631 of 7 December 2012: EO 13562 of 30 September 2013.

Notes:

EO 13543: National commission on the BP Deepwater Horizon Oil spill and offshore drilling: Two pages, signed 21 May 2010: Published 26 May 2010.

Notes:

EO 13542: providing an order of succession within the department of agriculture: Two pages, signed 13 May 2010: Published 18 May 2010: revokes: 13241 of 18 December 2001.

Notes:

EO 13541: temporary organization to facilitate a strategic partnership with the Republic of Iraq: Two pages, signed 7 May 2010: Published 12 May 2010.

Notes:

EO 13540: interagency task force on veterans small business development: Two pages, signed 26 April 2010: Published 29 April 2010: continued by: EO 13652 of 30 September 2013: Supersedes: EO 13299 of 8 May 2003.

Notes:

EO 13539: president's Council of advisors on science and technology: Three pages, signed 21 April 2010: Published 27 April 2010: revokes: 13226 of 30 September 2001.

Notes:

EO 13538: establishing the president's management advisory board: Two pages, signed 19 April 2010: Published 22 April 2010: amended by: EO 13652 of 30 September 2013.

Notes:

EO 13537: inter-agency group on insular areas: Two pages, signed 14 April 2010: Published 19 April 2010: supersedes: EO 13299 of 8 May 2003.

Notes:

EO 13536: blocking property of certain persons contributing to the conflict in Somalia: Four pages, signed 12 April 2010: Published 15 April 2010: see: EO 13620 of 20 July 2012.

Notes:

EO 13535: ensuring enforcement and implementation of abortion restrictions in the patient protection and affordable care act: Four pages, signed 24 March 2010: Published 29 March 2010.

Notes:

EO 13534: National export initiative: 3 pages, signed 11 March 2010: Published 15 March 2010: See: EO 12870 of 30 September 1993: EO 13630 of 6 December 2012

Notes:

EO 13533: providing an order of succession within the department of defense: Two pages, signed 1 March 2010: Published 5 March 2010: revokes: EO 13394 of 22 December 2005.

Notes:

EO 13532: promoting excellence, innovation, and sustainability at historically Black colleges and universities: Six pages, signed 26 February 2010: Published 3 March 2010: See: EO 13591 of 23 November 2011.

Notes:

EO 13531: National commission on fiscal responsibility and reform: Two pages, signed 18 February 2010: Published 23 February 2010.

Notes:

EO 13530: president's advisory Council on financial capability: Three pages, signed 29 January 2010: Published 3 February 2010: amended: EO 13591 of 23 November 2011.

Notes:

EO 13529: ordering the selected reserve and certain individual ready reserve members of the Armed Forces to active duty: One page, signed 16 January 2010: Published 21 January 2010.

Notes:

EO 13528: establishment of the council of governors: Two pages, signed 11 January 2010: Published 14 January 2010.

Notes:

EO 13527: establishing Federal capacity for the timely provision of medical countermeasures following a biological attack: Two pages, signed 30 December 2009: Published 6 January 2010.

Notes:

EO 13526: classified national security information: 27 pages, signed 29 December 2009: Published 5 January 2010: revokes: EO 12958 of 17 April 1995 EO 13525: Correction: One page, signed: Published 8 January 2010.

Notes:

Chapter 8: In the year 2009

In 2009 the president Published 39 executive orders EO 13489 through EO 15323:

EO 15323: half-day closing of executive departments and agencies on Thursday, December 24, 2009: 1 page, signed 11 December 2009: Published 16 December 2009.

Notes:

EO 13525: adjustments of certain rates of pay: 12 pages, signed 23 December 2009: Published 30 December 2009.

Notes:

EO 13524: amending executive order 12425 designating Interpol as a public international organization entitled to enjoy certain privileges, exemptions, and immunities: one page, signed 16

December 2009: Published 21 December 2009: Amends: EO 12425 of 16 June 1983: EO 13523: correction: signed: Published 18 December 2009.

Notes:

EO 13522: creating labor management forums to improve delivery of government services: Four pages, signed 9 December 2009: Published 14 December 2009: See: EO 13591 of 23 November 2011.

Notes:

EO 13521: establishing the presidential commission for the study of bioethical issues: Three pages, signed 24 November 2009: Published 30 November 2009: Continued by: EO 13652 of 30 September 2013.

Notes:

EO 13520: reducing improper payments: Five pages, signed 20 November 2009: Published 25 November 2009.

Notes:

EO 13519: establishment of the Financial fraud enforcement task force: Three pages, signed 17 November 2009: Published 19 November 2009: terminates: EO 13271 of 9 July 2002.

Notes:

EO 13518: employment of veterans in the federal government: Four pages, signed 9 November 2009: Published 13 November 2009: see: EO 13583 of 18 August 2011.

Notes:

EO 13517: amendments to executive orders 13183 and 13494: 2 pages, signed 30 October 2009: Published 5 November 2009: Amends: EO 13183 of 23 December 2000: EO 13494 of January 2009: EO 13516: correction: One page, signed: Published 5 November 2009.

Notes:

EO 13516: amending EO 13462: 2 pages, signed 28 October 2009: Published 2 November 2009: Federal register corrections.

Notes:

EO 13515: increasing participation of Asian Americans and Pacific islanders in federal programs: Four pages, signed 14 October 2009: Published 19 October 2009: supersedes: EO 13125 of 7 June 1999: EO 13339 of 13 May 2004: Amends: EO 13585 of 30 September 2011: EO 13652 of 30 September 2013 Continued by: EO 13652 of 30 September 2013.
Notes:

EO 13514: Federal leadership in environmental, energy, and economic performance: 11 pages, signed 5 October 2009: Published 8 November 2009: See: EO 13423 of 24 January 2007: EO 13677 of 23 September 2014: Revoked by: EO 13693 of 25 March 2015.

Notes:

EO 13513: Federal leadership on reducing text messaging while driving: Three pages, signed 1 October 2009: Published 6 October 2009.

Notes:

EO 13512: amending executive order 13390: 1 page, signed 29 September 2009: Published 2 October 2009: amends: EO 13390 of 1 November 2005.
Notes:

EO 13511: continuance of certain federal advisory committees: Two pages, signed 29 September 2009: Published 1 October 2009: continues: EO 11145 of 7 March 1964: EO 11183 of 3 October 1964.

Notes:

EO 13510: waiver under the trade act of 1974 with respect to the republic of Belarus: One page, signed 1 July 2009: Published 6 July 2009.

Notes:

EO 13509: establishing a White House council on automotive communities and workers: Three pages, signed 23 June 2009: Published 26 June 2009: Revoked by: EO 13578 of 6 July 2011.

Notes:

EO 13508: Chesapeake Bay protection and restoration: Six pages, signed 12 May 2009: Published 15 May 2009:

EO 13507: Establishment of the White House office of health reform: Three pages, signed 8 April 2009: Published 13 April 2009: revoked by: EO 13569 of 5 April 2011.

Notes:

EO 13506: establishing a White House Council on women and girls: Three pages, signed 11 March 2009: Published 16 March 2009.

Notes:

EO 13505: removing barriers to responsible scientific research involving human stem cells: Two pages, signed 9 March 2009: Published 11 March 2009: Revokes: EO 13435 of 20 June 2007.

Notes:

EO 13504: amending executive order 13390: 1 page, signed 20 February 2009: Published 24 February 2009: amends: EO 13390 of 1 November 2005.

Notes:

EO 13503: establishment of the White House office of urban affairs: Two pages, signed 19 February 2009: Published 24 February 2009.

Notes:

EO 13502: use of project labor agreements for federal construction Projects: three pages, signed 6 February 2009: Published 11 February 2009: Revokes: EO 13202 of 17 February 2001: EO 13208 of 6 April 2001.

Notes:

EO 13501: establishment of the president's economic recovery advisory board: Two pages, signed 6 February 2009: Published 11 February 2009: Revoked by: EO 13564 of 31 January 2011.

Notes:

EO 13500: further amendments to executive order 12859, establishment of the domestic policy Council: One page, signed 5 February 2009: Published 11 February 2009: Amends: EO 12859 of 16 August 1993.

Notes:

EO 13499: further amendments to executive order 12835, Establishment of the national economic Council: One page, signed 5 February 2009: Published 11 February 2009: Amends: EO 12835 of 25 January 1993.

Notes:

EO 13498: amendments to executive order 13199 and establishment of the president's advisory Council for faith based and neighborhood partnerships: 3 pages, signed 5 February 2009: Published 9 February 2009: amends: EO 13199 of 29 July 2001: see: EO 13559 of 17 November 2010: EO 13569 of 5 April 2011: EO 13640 of 5 April 2013: EO 13652 of 30 September 2013.

Notes:

EO 13497: revocation of certain executive orders concerning regulatory planning and review: One page, signed 30 January 2009: Published 4 February 2009: Revokes: EO 13258 of 26 February 2002: EO 13422 of 18 January 2007: See: EO 12866 of 30 September 1993.

Notes:

EO 13496: Notification of employee rights under federal labor laws: Five pages, signed 30 January

2009: Published 4 February 2009: revokes: EO 13201 of 17 February 2001.

Notes:

EO 13495: non-displacement of qualified workers under service contracts: Four pages, signed 30 January 2009: Published 4 February 2009: revokes: EO 13204 of 17 February 2001.

Notes:

EO 13494: economy in government contracting: Two pages, signed 30 January 2009: Published 4 February 2009: amends: EO 13517 of 30 October 2009.

Notes:

EO 13493: review of detention policy options: Two pages, signed 22 January 2009: Published 27 January 2009.

Notes:

EO 13492: review and disposition of individuals detained at the Guantánamo Bay Naval base and closure of detention facilities: Four pages, signed 22 January 2009: Published 27 January 2009: See: EO 13567 of 7 March 2011.

Notes:

EO 13491: ensuring lawful interrogations: Four pages, signed 22 January 2009: Published 27 January 2009: see: EO 13567 of 7 March 2011: revokes: EO 13440 of 20 July 2007.

Notes:

EO 13490: Ethics commitments by executive branch personnel: Six pages, signed 21 January 2009: Published 26 January 2009.

Notes:

EO 13489: Presidential records: Three pages, signed 21 January 2009: Published 26 January 2009: Revokes: EO 13233 of 1 November 2001.

Notes:

Chapter 9: The Declaration of Independence

(Source: https://www.archives.gov/exhibits/charters/)

IN CONGRESS, July 4, 1776.
The unanimous Declaration of the thirteen united States of America,
When in the Course of human events, it becomes necessary for one people to dissolve the political bands which have connected them with another, and to assume among the powers of the earth, the separate and equal station to which the Laws of Nature and of Nature's God entitle them, a decent respect to the opinions of mankind requires that they should declare the causes which impel them to the separation. We hold these truths to be self-evident, that all men are created equal, that they are endowed by their Creator with certain unalienable Rights, that among these are Life, Liberty and the pursuit of Happiness.--That to secure these rights, Governments are instituted among Men, deriving their just powers from the consent of the governed, --That whenever any Form of Government becomes destructive of these ends, it is the Right of the People to alter or to abolish it, and to institute new Government, laying its foundation on such principles and organizing its powers in such form, as to them shall seem most likely to effect their Safety and Happiness. Prudence, indeed, will dictate that Governments long established should not be changed for light and transient causes; and accordingly all experience hath shewn, that mankind are more disposed to suffer, while evils are sufferable, than to right themselves by abolishing the forms to which they are accustomed. But when a long train of abuses and usurpations, pursuing invariably the same Object evinces a design to reduce them under absolute Despotism, it is their right, it is their duty, to throw off such Government, and to provide new Guards for their future security.--Such has been the patient sufferance of these Colonies; and such is now the necessity which constrains them to alter their former Systems of Government. The history of the present King of Great Britain is a history of repeated injuries and usurpations, all having in direct object the establishment of an absolute Tyranny over these States. To prove this, let Facts be submitted to a candid world.

> *He has refused his Assent to Laws, the most wholesome and necessary for the public good.*
> *He has forbidden his Governors to pass Laws of immediate and*

pressing importance, unless suspended in their operation till his Assent should be obtained; and when so suspended, he has utterly neglected to attend to them.

He has refused to pass other Laws for the accommodation of large districts of people, unless those people would relinquish the right of Representation in the Legislature, a right inestimable to them and formidable to tyrants only.

He has called together legislative bodies at places unusual, uncomfortable, and distant from the depository of their public Records, for the sole purpose of fatiguing them into compliance with his measures.

He has dissolved Representative Houses repeatedly, for opposing with manly firmness his invasions on the rights of the people.

He has refused for a long time, after such dissolutions, to cause others to be elected; whereby the Legislative powers, incapable of Annihilation, have returned to the People at large for their exercise; the State remaining in the mean time exposed to all the dangers of invasion from without, and convulsions within.

He has endeavoured to prevent the population of these States; for that purpose obstructing the Laws for Naturalization of Foreigners; refusing to pass others to encourage their migrations hither, and raising the conditions of new Appropriations of Lands.

He has obstructed the Administration of Justice, by refusing his Assent to Laws for establishing Judiciary powers.

He has made Judges dependent on his Will alone, for the tenure of their offices, and the amount and payment of their salaries.

He has erected a multitude of New Offices, and sent hither swarms of Officers to harrass our people, and eat out their substance.

He has kept among us, in times of peace, Standing Armies without the Consent of our legislatures.

He has affected to render the Military independent of and superior to the Civil power.

He has combined with others to subject us to a jurisdiction foreign to our constitution, and unacknowledged by our laws; giving his Assent to their Acts of pretended Legislation:

For Quartering large bodies of armed troops among us:

For protecting them, by a mock Trial, from punishment for any

Murders which they should commit on the Inhabitants of these States:

For cutting off our Trade with all parts of the world:

For imposing Taxes on us without our Consent:

For depriving us in many cases, of the benefits of Trial by Jury:

For transporting us beyond Seas to be tried for pretended offences

For abolishing the free System of English Laws in a neighbouring Province, establishing therein an Arbitrary government, and enlarging its Boundaries so as to render it at once an example and fit instrument for introducing the same absolute rule into these Colonies:

For taking away our Charters, abolishing our most valuable Laws, and altering fundamentally the Forms of our Governments:

For suspending our own Legislatures, and declaring themselves invested with power to legislate for us in all cases whatsoever.

He has abdicated Government here, by declaring us out of his Protection and waging War against us.

He has plundered our seas, ravaged our Coasts, burnt our towns, and destroyed the lives of our people.

He is at this time transporting large Armies of foreign Mercenaries to compleat the works of death, desolation and tyranny, already begun with circumstances of Cruelty & perfidy scarcely paralleled in the most barbarous ages, and totally unworthy the Head of a civilized nation.

He has constrained our fellow Citizens taken Captive on the high Seas to bear Arms against their Country, to become the executioners of their friends and Brethren, or to fall themselves by their Hands.

He has excited domestic insurrections amongst us, and has endeavoured to bring on the inhabitants of our frontiers, the merciless Indian Savages, whose known rule of warfare, is an undistinguished destruction of all ages, sexes and conditions.

In every stage of these Oppressions We have Petitioned for Redress in the most humble terms: Our repeated Petitions have been answered only by repeated injury. A Prince whose character is thus marked by every act which may define a Tyrant, is unfit to be the ruler of a free people.

Nor have We been wanting in attentions to our Brittish brethren. We have warned them from time to time of attempts by their legislature to extend an unwarrantable jurisdiction over us. We have reminded them of the circumstances of our emigration and settlement here. We have appealed to their native justice and magnanimity, and we have conjured them by the ties of our common kindred to disavow these usurpations, which, would inevitably interrupt our connections and correspondence. They too have been deaf to the voice of justice and of consanguinity. We must, therefore, acquiesce in the necessity, which denounces our Separation, and hold them, as we hold the rest of mankind, Enemies in War, in Peace Friends.

We, therefore, the Representatives of the united States of America, in General Congress, Assembled, appealing to the Supreme Judge of the world for the rectitude of our intentions, do, in the Name, and by Authority of the good People of these Colonies, solemnly publish and declare, That these United Colonies are, and of Right ought to be Free and Independent States; that they are Absolved from all Allegiance to the British Crown, and that all political connection between them and the State of Great Britain, is and ought to be totally dissolved; and that as Free and Independent States, they have full Power to levy War, conclude Peace, contract Alliances, establish Commerce, and to do all other Acts and Things which Independent States may of right do. And for the support of this Declaration, with a firm reliance on the protection of divine Providence, we mutually pledge to each other our Lives, our Fortunes and our sacred Honor.

The 56 signatures on the Declaration appear in the positions indicated,

Column 3
Massachusetts:
John Hancock
Maryland:
Samuel Chase
William Paca
Thomas Stone
Charles Carroll of Carrollton
Virginia:
George Wythe
Richard Henry Lee
Thomas Jefferson
Benjamin Harrison
Thomas Nelson, Jr.

Francis Lightfoot Lee
Carter Braxton

Column 4
Pennsylvania:
  Robert Morris
  Benjamin Rush
  Benjamin Franklin
  John Morton
  George Clymer
  James Smith
  George Taylor
  James Wilson
  George Ross
Delaware:
  Caesar Rodney
  George Read
  Thomas McKean

Column 5
New York:
  William Floyd
  Philip Livingston
  Francis Lewis
  Lewis Morris
New Jersey:
  Richard Stockton
  John Witherspoon
  Francis Hopkinson
  John Hart
  Abraham Clark

Column 6
New Hampshire:
  Josiah Bartlett
  William Whipple
Massachusetts:
  Samuel Adams
  John Adams
  Robert Treat Paine
  Elbridge Gerry
Rhode Island:
  Stephen Hopkins
  William Ellery

Connecticut:
  Roger Sherman
  Samuel Huntington
  William Williams
  Oliver Wolcott
New Hampshire:
  Matthew Thornton

Chapter 10: The United States Constitution

(Source:http://www.archives.gov/exhibits/charters/constitution_transcript.html)

We the People of the United States, in Order to form a more perfect Union, establish Justice, insure domestic Tranquility, provide for the common defence, promote the general Welfare, and secure the Blessings of Liberty to ourselves and our Posterity, do ordain and establish this Constitution for the United States of America.

Article. I.

Section. 1.

All legislative Powers herein granted shall be vested in a Congress of the United States, which shall consist of a Senate and House of Representatives.

Section. 2.

The House of Representatives shall be composed of Members chosen every second Year by the People of the several States, and the Electors in each State shall have the Qualifications requisite for Electors of the most numerous Branch of the State Legislature.

No Person shall be a Representative who shall not have attained to the Age of twenty five Years, and been seven Years a Citizen of the United States, and who shall not, when elected, be an Inhabitant of that State in which he shall be chosen.

Representatives and direct Taxes shall be apportioned among the several States which may be included within this Union, according to their respective Numbers, which shall be determined by adding to the whole Number of free Persons, including those bound to Service for a Term of Years, and excluding Indians not taxed, three fifths of all other Persons. The actual Enumeration shall be made within three Years after the first Meeting of the Congress of the United States, and within every subsequent Term of ten Years, in such Manner as they shall by Law direct. The Number of Representatives shall not exceed one for every thirty Thousand, but each State shall have at Least one Representative; and until such enumeration shall be made, the State of New Hampshire shall be entitled to chuse three, Massachusetts eight, Rhode-Island and Providence Plantations one, Connecticut five, New-York six, New Jersey four, Pennsylvania eight, Delaware one, Maryland six, Virginia ten, North Carolina five, South Carolina five, and Georgia three.

When vacancies happen in the Representation from any State, the Executive Authority thereof shall issue Writs of Election to fill such Vacancies.

The House of Representatives shall chuse their Speaker and other Officers; and shall have the sole Power of Impeachment.

Section. 3.

The Senate of the United States shall be composed of two Senators from each State, Legislature thereof, for six Years; and each Senator shall have one Vote.

Immediately after they shall be assembled in Consequence of the first Election, they shall be divided as equally as may be into three Classes. The Seats of the Senators of the first Class shall be vacated at the Expiration of the second Year, of the second Class at the Expiration of the fourth Year, and of the third Class at the Expiration of the sixth Year, so that one third may be chosen every second Year; <u>*and if Vacancies happen by Resignation, or otherwise, during the Recess of the Legislature of any State, the Executive thereof may make temporary Appointments until the next Meeting of the Legislature, which shall then fill such Vacancies.*</u>

No Person shall be a Senator who shall not have attained to the Age of thirty Years, and been nine Years a Citizen of the United States, and who shall not, when elected, be an Inhabitant of that State for which he shall be chosen.

The Vice President of the United States shall be President of the Senate, but shall have no Vote, unless they be equally divided.

The Senate shall chuse their other Officers, and also a President pro tempore, in the Absence of the Vice President, or when he shall exercise the Office of President of the United States.

The Senate shall have the sole Power to try all Impeachments. When sitting for that Purpose, they shall be on Oath or Affirmation. When the President of the United States is tried, the Chief Justice shall preside: And no Person shall be convicted without the Concurrence of two thirds of the Members present.

Judgment in Cases of Impeachment shall not extend further than to removal from Office, and disqualification to hold and enjoy any Office of honor, Trust or Profit under the United States: but the Party convicted shall nevertheless be liable and subject to Indictment, Trial, Judgment and Punishment, according to Law.

Section. 4.

The Times, Places and Manner of holding Elections for Senators and Representatives, shall be prescribed in each State by the Legislature thereof; but the Congress may at any time by Law make or alter such Regulations, except as to the Places of chusing Senators.

The Congress shall assemble at least once in every Year, and such Meeting shall _be on the first Monday in December_, unless they shall by Law appoint a different Day.

Section. 5.

Each House shall be the Judge of the Elections, Returns and Qualifications of its own Members, and a Majority of each shall constitute a Quorum to do Business; but a smaller Number may adjourn from day to day, and may be authorized to compel the Attendance of absent Members, in such Manner, and under such Penalties as each House may provide.

Each House may determine the Rules of its Proceedings, punish its Members for disorderly Behaviour, and, with the Concurrence of two thirds, expel a Member.

Each House shall keep a Journal of its Proceedings, and from time to time publish the same, excepting such Parts as may in their Judgment require Secrecy; and the Yeas and Nays of the Members of either House on any question shall, at the Desire of one fifth of those Present, be entered on the Journal.

Neither House, during the Session of Congress, shall, without the Consent of the other, adjourn for more than three days, nor to any other Place than that in which the two Houses shall be sitting.

Section. 6.

The Senators and Representatives shall receive a Compensation for their Services, to be ascertained by Law, and paid out of the Treasury of the United States. They shall in all Cases, except Treason, Felony and Breach of the Peace, be privileged from Arrest during their Attendance at the Session of their respective Houses, and in going to and returning from the same; and for any Speech or Debate in either House, they shall not be questioned in any other Place.

No Senator or Representative shall, during the Time for which he was elected, be appointed to any civil Office under the Authority of the United States, which shall have been created, or the Emoluments whereof shall have been encreased during such time; and no Person holding any Office under the United States, shall be a Member of either House during his Continuance in Office.

Section. 7.

All Bills for raising Revenue shall originate in the House of Representatives; but the Senate may propose or concur with Amendments as on other Bills.

Every Bill which shall have passed the House of Representatives and the Senate, shall, before it become a Law, be presented to the President of the United States; If he approve he shall sign it, but if not he shall return it, with his Objections to that House in which it shall have originated, who shall enter the Objections at large on their Journal, and proceed to reconsider it. If after such Reconsideration two thirds of that House shall agree to pass the Bill, it shall be sent, together with the Objections, to the other House, by which it shall likewise be reconsidered, and if approved by two thirds of that House, it shall become a Law. But in all such Cases the Votes of both Houses shall be determined by yeas and Nays, and the Names of the Persons voting for and against the Bill shall be entered on the Journal of each House respectively. If any Bill shall not be returned by the President within ten Days (Sundays excepted) after it shall have been presented to him, the Same shall be a Law, in like Manner as if he had signed it, unless the Congress by their Adjournment prevent its Return, in which Case it shall not be a Law.

Every Order, Resolution, or Vote to which the Concurrence of the Senate and House of Representatives may be necessary (except on a question of Adjournment) shall be presented to the President of the United States; and before the Same shall take Effect, shall be approved by him, or being disapproved by him, shall be repassed by two thirds of the Senate and House of Representatives, according to the Rules and Limitations prescribed in the Case of a Bill.

Section. 8.

The Congress shall have Power To lay and collect Taxes, Duties, Imposts and Excises, to pay the Debts and provide for the common Defence and general Welfare of the United States; but all Duties, Imposts and Excises shall be uniform throughout the United States;

To borrow Money on the credit of the United States;

To regulate Commerce with foreign Nations, and among the several States, and with the Indian Tribes;

To establish an uniform Rule of Naturalization, and uniform Laws on the subject of Bankruptcies throughout the United States;

To coin Money, regulate the Value thereof, and of foreign Coin, and fix the Standard of Weights and Measures;

To provide for the Punishment of counterfeiting the Securities and current Coin of the United States;

To establish Post Offices and post Roads;

To promote the Progress of Science and useful Arts, by securing for limited Times to Authors and Inventors the exclusive Right to their respective Writings and Discoveries;

To constitute Tribunals inferior to the supreme Court;

To define and punish Piracies and Felonies committed on the high Seas, and Offences against the Law of Nations;

To declare War, grant Letters of Marque and Reprisal, and make Rules concerning Captures on Land and Water;

To raise and support Armies, but no Appropriation of Money to that Use shall be for a longer Term than two Years;

To provide and maintain a Navy;

To make Rules for the Government and Regulation of the land and naval Forces;

To provide for calling forth the Militia to execute the Laws of the Union, suppress Insurrections and repel Invasions;

To provide for organizing, arming, and disciplining, the Militia, and for governing such Part of them as may be employed in the Service of the United States, reserving to the States respectively, the Appointment of the Officers, and the Authority of training the Militia according to the discipline prescribed by Congress;

To exercise exclusive Legislation in all Cases whatsoever, over such District (not exceeding ten Miles square) as may, by Cession of particular States, and the Acceptance of Congress, become the Seat of the Government of the United States, and to exercise like Authority over all Places purchased by the Consent of the Legislature of the State in which the Same shall be, for the Erection of Forts, Magazines, Arsenals, dock-Yards, and other needful Buildings;—And

To make all Laws which shall be necessary and proper for carrying into Execution the foregoing Powers, and all other Powers vested by this Constitution in the Government of the United States, or in any Department or Officer thereof.

Section. 9.

The Migration or Importation of such Persons as any of the States now existing shall think proper to admit, shall not be prohibited by the Congress prior to the Year one thousand eight hundred and eight, but a Tax or duty may be imposed on such Importation, not exceeding ten dollars for each Person.

The Privilege of the Writ of Habeas Corpus shall not be suspended, unless when in Cases of Rebellion or Invasion the public Safety may require it.

No Bill of Attainder or ex post facto Law shall be passed.

No Capitation, or other direct, Tax shall be laid, unless in Proportion to the Census or enumeration herein before directed to be taken.

No Tax or Duty shall be laid on Articles exported from any State.

No Preference shall be given by any Regulation of Commerce or Revenue to the Ports of one State over those of another: nor shall Vessels bound to, or from, one State, be obliged to enter, clear, or pay Duties in another.

No Money shall be drawn from the Treasury, but in Consequence of Appropriations made by Law; and a regular Statement and Account of the Receipts and Expenditures of all public Money shall be published from time to time.

No Title of Nobility shall be granted by the United States: And no Person holding any Office of Profit or Trust under them, shall, without the Consent of the Congress, accept of any present, Emolument, Office, or Title, of any kind whatever, from any King, Prince, or foreign State.

Section. 10.

No State shall enter into any Treaty, Alliance, or Confederation; grant Letters of Marque and Reprisal; coin Money; emit Bills of Credit; make any Thing but gold and silver Coin a Tender in Payment of Debts; pass any Bill of Attainder, ex post facto Law, or Law impairing the Obligation of Contracts, or grant any Title of Nobility.

No State shall, without the Consent of the Congress, lay any Imposts or Duties on Imports or Exports, except what may be absolutely necessary for executing it's inspection Laws: and the net Produce of all Duties and Imposts, laid by any State on Imports or Exports, shall be for the Use of the Treasury of the United States; and all such Laws shall be subject to the Revision and Controul of the Congress.

No State shall, without the Consent of Congress, lay any Duty of Tonnage, keep Troops, or Ships of War in time of Peace, enter into any Agreement or Compact with another State, or with a foreign Power, or engage in War, unless actually invaded, or in such imminent Danger as will not admit of delay.

Article. II.

Section. 1.

The executive Power shall be vested in a President of the United States of America. He shall hold his Office during the Term of four Years, and, together with the Vice President, chosen for the same Term, be elected, as follows

Each State shall appoint, in such Manner as the Legislature thereof may direct, a Number of Electors, equal to the whole Number of Senators and Representatives to which the State may be entitled in the Congress: but no Senator or Representative, or Person holding an

Office of Trust or Profit under the United States, shall be appointed an Elector.

The Electors shall meet in their respective States, and vote by Ballot for two Persons, of whom one at least shall not be an Inhabitant of the same State with themselves. And they shall make a List of all the Persons voted for, and of the Number of Votes for each; which List they shall sign and certify, and transmit sealed to the Seat of the Government of the United States, directed to the President of the Senate. The President of the Senate shall, in the Presence of the Senate and House of Representatives, open all the Certificates, and the Votes shall then be counted. The Person having the greatest Number of Votes shall be the President, if such Number be a Majority of the whole Number of Electors appointed; and if there be more than one who have such Majority, and have an equal Number of Votes, then the House of Representatives shall immediately chuse by Ballot one of them for President; and if no Person have a Majority, then from the five highest on the List the said House shall in like Manner chuse the President. But in chusing the President, the Votes shall be taken by States, the Representation from each State having one Vote; A quorum for this Purpose shall consist of a Member or Members from two thirds of the States, and a Majority of all the States shall be necessary to a Choice. In every Case, after the Choice of the President, the Person having the greatest Number of Votes of the Electors shall be the Vice President. But if there should remain two or more who have equal Votes, the Senate shall chuse from them by Ballot the Vice President.

The Congress may determine the Time of chusing the Electors, and the Day on which they shall give their Votes; which Day shall be the same throughout the United States.

No Person except a natural born Citizen, or a Citizen of the United States, at the time of the Adoption of this Constitution, shall be eligible to the Office of President; neither shall any Person be eligible to that Office who shall not have attained to the Age of thirty five Years, and been fourteen Years a Resident within the United States.

In Case of the Removal of the President from Office, or of his Death, Resignation, or Inability to discharge the Powers and Duties of the said Office, the Same shall devolve on the Vice President, and the Congress

may by Law provide for the Case of Removal, Death, Resignation or
Inability, both of the President and Vice President, declaring what
Officer shall then act as President, and such Officer shall act
accordingly, until the Disability be removed, or a President shall be
elected.

The President shall, at stated Times, receive for his Services, a
Compensation, which shall neither be encreased nor diminished during
the Period for which he shall have been elected, and he shall not
receive within that Period any other Emolument from the United States,
or any of them.

Before he enter on the Execution of his Office, he shall take the
following Oath or Affirmation:—"I do solemnly swear (or affirm) that I
will faithfully execute the Office of President of the United States, and
will to the best of my Ability, preserve, protect and defend the
Constitution of the United States."

Section. 2.

The President shall be Commander in Chief of the Army and Navy of
the United States, and of the Militia of the several States, when called
into the actual Service of the United States; he may require the
Opinion, in writing, of the principal Officer in each of the executive
Departments, upon any Subject relating to the Duties of their respective
Offices, and he shall have Power to grant Reprieves and Pardons for
Offences against the United States, except in Cases of Impeachment.

He shall have Power, by and with the Advice and Consent of the
Senate, to make Treaties, provided two thirds of the Senators present
concur; and he shall nominate, and by and with the Advice and
Consent of the Senate, shall appoint Ambassadors, other public
Ministers and Consuls, Judges of the supreme Court, and all other
Officers of the United States, whose Appointments are not herein
otherwise provided for, and which shall be established by Law: but the
Congress may by Law vest the Appointment of such inferior Officers, as
they think proper, in the President alone, in the Courts of Law, or in
the Heads of Departments.

The President shall have Power to fill up all Vacancies that may happen during the Recess of the Senate, by granting Commissions which shall expire at the End of their next Session.

Section. 3.

He shall from time to time give to the Congress Information of the State of the Union, and recommend to their Consideration such Measures as he shall judge necessary and expedient; he may, on extraordinary Occasions, convene both Houses, or either of them, and in Case of Disagreement between them, with Respect to the Time of Adjournment, he may adjourn them to such Time as he shall think proper; he shall receive Ambassadors and other public Ministers; he shall take Care that the Laws be faithfully executed, and shall Commission all the Officers of the United States.

Section. 4.

The President, Vice President and all civil Officers of the United States, shall be removed from Office on Impeachment for, and Conviction of, Treason, Bribery, or other high Crimes and Misdemeanors.

Article III.

Section. 1.

The judicial Power of the United States, shall be vested in one supreme Court, and in such inferior Courts as the Congress may from time to time ordain and establish. The Judges, both of the supreme and inferior Courts, shall hold their Offices during good Behaviour, and shall, at stated Times, receive for their Services, a Compensation, which shall not be diminished during their Continuance in Office.

Section. 2.

The judicial Power shall extend to all Cases, in Law and Equity, arising under this Constitution, the Laws of the United States, and Treaties made, or which shall be made, under their Authority;—to all

Cases affecting Ambassadors, other public Ministers and Consuls;—to all Cases of admiralty and maritime Jurisdiction;—to Controversies to which the United States shall be a Party;—to Controversies between two or more States;—*between a State and Citizens of another State*,—between Citizens of different States,—between Citizens of the same State claiming Lands under Grants of different States, and between a State, or the Citizens thereof, and foreign States, Citizens or Subjects.

In all Cases affecting Ambassadors, other public Ministers and Consuls, and those in which a State shall be Party, the supreme Court shall have original Jurisdiction. In all the other Cases before mentioned, the supreme Court shall have appellate Jurisdiction, both as to Law and Fact, with such Exceptions, and under such Regulations as the Congress shall make.

The Trial of all Crimes, except in Cases of Impeachment, shall be by Jury; and such Trial shall be held in the State where the said Crimes shall have been committed; but when not committed within any State, the Trial shall be at such Place or Places as the Congress may by Law have directed.

Section. 3.

Treason against the United States, shall consist only in levying War against them, or in adhering to their Enemies, giving them Aid and Comfort. No Person shall be convicted of Treason unless on the Testimony of two Witnesses to the same overt Act, or on Confession in open Court.

The Congress shall have Power to declare the Punishment of Treason, but no Attainder of Treason shall work Corruption of Blood, or Forfeiture except during the Life of the Person attainted.

Article. IV.

Section. 1.

Full Faith and Credit shall be given in each State to the public Acts, Records, and judicial Proceedings of every other State. And the Congress may by general Laws prescribe the Manner in which such Acts, Records and Proceedings shall be proved, and the Effect thereof.

Section. 2.

The Citizens of each State shall be entitled to all Privileges and Immunities of Citizens in the several States.

A Person charged in any State with Treason, Felony, or other Crime, who shall flee from Justice, and be found in another State, shall on Demand of the executive Authority of the State from which he fled, be delivered up, to be removed to the State having Jurisdiction of the Crime.

No Person held to Service or Labour in one State, under the Laws thereof, escaping into another, shall, in Consequence of any Law or Regulation therein, be discharged from such Service or Labour, but shall be delivered up on Claim of the Party to whom such Service or Labour may be due.

Section. 3.

New States may be admitted by the Congress into this Union; but no new State shall be formed or erected within the Jurisdiction of any other State; nor any State be formed by the Junction of two or more States, or Parts of States, without the Consent of the Legislatures of the States concerned as well as of the Congress.

The Congress shall have Power to dispose of and make all needful Rules and Regulations respecting the Territory or other Property belonging to the United States; and nothing in this Constitution shall be so construed as to Prejudice any Claims of the United States, or of any particular State.

Section. 4.

The United States shall guarantee to every State in this Union a Republican Form of Government, and shall protect each of them *against Invasion; and on Application of the Legislature, or of the Executive (when the Legislature cannot be convened), against domestic Violence.*

Article. V.

The Congress, whenever two thirds of both Houses shall deem it necessary, shall propose Amendments to this Constitution, or, on the Application of the Legislatures of two thirds of the several States, shall call a Convention for proposing Amendments, which, in either Case, shall be valid to all Intents and Purposes, as Part of this Constitution, when ratified by the Legislatures of three fourths of the several States, or by Conventions in three fourths thereof, as the one or the other Mode of Ratification may be proposed by the Congress; Provided that no Amendment which may be made prior to the Year One thousand eight hundred and eight shall in any Manner affect the first and fourth Clauses in the Ninth Section of the first Article; and that no State, without its Consent, shall be deprived of its equal Suffrage in the Senate.

Article. VI.

All Debts contracted and Engagements entered into, before the Adoption of this Constitution, shall be as valid against the United States under this Constitution, as under the Confederation.

This Constitution, and the Laws of the United States which shall be made in Pursuance thereof; and all Treaties made, or which shall be made, under the Authority of the United States, shall be the supreme Law of the Land; and the Judges in every State shall be bound thereby, any Thing in the Constitution or Laws of any State to the Contrary notwithstanding.

The Senators and Representatives before mentioned, and the Members of the several State Legislatures, and all executive and judicial Officers, both of the United States and of the several States, shall be bound by Oath or Affirmation, to support this Constitution; but no religious Test shall ever be required as a Qualification to any Office or public Trust under the United States.

Article. VII.

The Ratification of the Conventions of nine States, shall be sufficient for the Establishment of this Constitution between the States so ratifying the Same.

The Word, "the," being interlined between the seventh and eighth Lines of the first Page, The Word "Thirty" being partly written on an Erazure in the fifteenth Line of the first Page, The Words "is tried" being interlined between the thirty second and thirty third Lines of the first Page and the Word "the" being interlined between the forty third and forty fourth Lines of the second Page.

Attest William Jackson Secretary

done in Convention by the Unanimous Consent of the States present the Seventeenth Day of September in the Year of our Lord one thousand seven hundred and Eighty seven and of the Independance of the United States of America the Twelfth In witness whereof We have hereunto subscribed our Names,

G°. Washington
Presidt and deputy from Virginia

Delaware
GEO: Read
Gunning Bedford jun
John Dickinson
Richard Bassett
Jaco: Broom

Maryland
James McHenry
Dan of St Thos. Jenifer
Danl. Carroll

Virginia
John Blair
James Madison Jr.

North Carolina
Wm. Blount
Richd. Dobbs Spaight
Hu Williamson

South Carolina
J. Rutledge
Charles Cotesworth Pinckney
Charles Pinckney
Pierce Butler

Georgia
William Few
Abr Baldwin

New Hampshire
John Langdon
Nicholas Gilman

Massachusetts
Nathaniel Gorham
Rufus King

Connecticut
Wm. Saml. Johnson
Roger Sherman

New York
Alexander Hamilton

New Jersey
Wil: Livingston
David Brearley
Wm. Paterson
Jona: Dayton

Pensylvania
B Franklin
GEO. Clymer
Thos. FitzSimons
Jared Ingersoll
James Wilson
Gouv Morris

Chapter 11: The Bill of Rights

(Source:http://www.archives.gov/exhibits/charters/bill_of_rights_transcript.html)

On September 25, 1789, the First Congress of the United States proposed 12 amendments to the Constitution. The 1789 Joint Resolution of Congress proposing the amendments is on display in the Rotunda in the National Archives Museum. Ten of the proposed 12 amendments were ratified by three-fourths of the state legislatures on December 15, 1791. The ratified Articles (Articles 3–12) constitute the first 10 amendments of the Constitution, or the U.S. Bill of Rights. In 1992, 203 years after it was proposed, Article 2 was ratified as the 27th Amendment to the Constitution. Article 1 was never ratified.

Transcription of the 1789 Joint Resolution of Congress Proposing 12 Amendments to the U.S. Constitution

Congress of the United States
begun and held at the City of New-York, on
Wednesday the fourth of March, one thousand seven hundred and eighty nine.

THE Conventions of a number of the States, having at the time of their adopting the Constitution, expressed a desire, in order to prevent misconstruction or abuse of its powers, that further declaratory and restrictive clauses should be added: And as extending the ground of public confidence in the Government, will best ensure the beneficent ends of its institution.
RESOLVED by the Senate and House of Representatives of the United States of America, in Congress assembled, two thirds of both Houses concurring, that the following Articles be proposed to the Legislatures of the several States, as amendments to the Constitution of the United States, all, or any of which Articles, when ratified by three fourths of the said Legislatures, to be valid to all intents and purposes, as part of the said Constitution; viz.

ARTICLES in addition to, and Amendment of the Constitution of the United States of America, proposed by Congress, and ratified by the Legislatures of the several States, pursuant to the fifth Article of the original Constitution.

Article the first... After the first enumeration required by the first article of the Constitution, there shall be one Representative for every thirty thousand, until the number shall amount to one hundred, after which the proportion shall be so regulated by Congress, that there shall be not less than one hundred Representatives, nor less than one Representative for every forty thousand persons, until the number of Representatives shall amount to two hundred; after which the proportion shall be so regulated by Congress, that there shall not be less than two hundred Representatives, nor more than one Representative for every fifty thousand persons.

Article the second... No law, varying the compensation for the services of the Senators and Representatives, shall take effect, until an election of Representatives shall have intervened.

Article the third... Congress shall make no law respecting an establishment of religion, or prohibiting the free exercise thereof; or abridging the freedom of speech, or of the press; or the right of the people peaceably to assemble, and to petition the Government for a redress of grievances.

Article the fourth... A well regulated Militia, being necessary to the security of a free State, the right of the people to keep and bear Arms, shall not be infringed.

Article the fifth... No Soldier shall, in time of peace be quartered in any house, without the consent of the Owner, nor in time of war, but in a manner to be prescribed by law.

Article the sixth... The right of the people to be secure in their persons, houses, papers, and effects, against unreasonable searches and seizures, shall not be violated, and no Warrants shall issue, but upon probable cause, supported by Oath or affirmation, and particularly describing the place to be searched, and the persons or things to be seized.

Article the seventh... No person shall be held to answer for a capital, or otherwise infamous crime, unless on a presentment or indictment of a Grand Jury, except in cases arising in the land or naval forces, or in the Militia, when in actual service in time of War or public danger; nor shall any person be subject for the same offence to be twice put in jeopardy of life or limb; nor shall be compelled in any criminal case to be a witness against himself, nor be deprived of life, liberty, or property, without due process of law; nor shall private property be taken for public use, without just compensation.

Article the eighth... In all criminal prosecutions, the accused shall enjoy the right to a speedy and public trial, by an impartial jury of the State and district wherein the crime shall have been committed, which district shall have been previously ascertained by law, and to be informed of the nature and cause of the accusation; to be confronted with the witnesses against him; to have compulsory process for obtaining witnesses in his favor, and to have the Assistance of Counsel for his defence.

Article the ninth... In suits at common law, where the value in controversy shall exceed twenty dollars, the right of trial by jury shall be preserved, and no fact tried by a jury, shall be otherwise re-examined in any Court of the United States, than according to the rules of the common law.

Article the tenth... Excessive bail shall not be required, nor excessive fines imposed, nor cruel and unusual punishments inflicted.

Article the eleventh... The enumeration in the Constitution, of certain rights, shall not be construed to deny or disparage others retained by the people.

Article the twelfth... The powers not delegated to the United States by the Constitution, nor prohibited by it to the States, are reserved to the States respectively, or to the people.

ATTEST,

Frederick Augustus Muhlenberg, Speaker of the House of Representatives

John Adams, Vice-President of the United States, and President of the Senate

John Beckley, Clerk of the House of Representatives.

Sam. A Otis Secretary of the Senate

Amendments 11-27

Note: The capitalization and punctuation in this version is from the enrolled original of the Joint Resolution of Congress proposing the Bill of Rights, which is on permanent display in the Rotunda of the National Archives Building, Washington, D.C.
The U.S. Bill of Rights
The Preamble to The Bill of Rights

Congress of the United States
begun and held at the City of New-York, on
Wednesday the fourth of March, one thousand seven hundred and eighty nine.

THE Conventions of a number of the States, having at the time of their adopting the Constitution, expressed a desire, in order to prevent misconstruction or abuse of its powers, that further declaratory and restrictive clauses should be added: And as extending the ground of public confidence in the Government, will best ensure the beneficent ends of its institution.

RESOLVED by the Senate and House of Representatives of the United States of America, in Congress assembled, two thirds of both Houses concurring, that the following Articles be proposed to the Legislatures of the several States, as amendments to the Constitution of the United States, all, or any of which Articles, when ratified by three fourths of the said Legislatures, to be valid to all intents and purposes, as part of the said Constitution; viz.

ARTICLES in addition to, and Amendment of the Constitution of the United States of America, proposed by Congress, and ratified by the Legislatures of the several States, pursuant to the fifth Article of the original Constitution.

Note: The following text is a transcription of the first ten amendments to the Constitution in their original form. These amendments were ratified December 15, 1791, and form what is known as the "Bill of Rights."

Amendment I

Congress shall make no law respecting an establishment of religion, or prohibiting the free exercise thereof; or abridging the freedom of speech, or of the press; or the right of the people peaceably to assemble, and to petition the Government for a redress of grievances.

Amendment II

A well regulated Militia, being necessary to the security of a free State, the right of the people to keep and bear Arms, shall not be infringed.

Amendment III

No Soldier shall, in time of peace be quartered in any house, without the consent of the Owner, nor in time of war, but in a manner to be prescribed by law.

Amendment IV

The right of the people to be secure in their persons, houses, papers, and effects, against unreasonable searches and seizures, shall not be violated, and no Warrants shall issue, but upon probable cause, supported by Oath or affirmation, and particularly describing the place to be searched, and the persons or things to be seized.

Amendment V

No person shall be held to answer for a capital, or otherwise infamous crime, unless on a presentment or indictment of a Grand Jury, except in cases arising in the land or naval forces, or in the Militia, when in actual service in time of War or public danger; nor shall any person be subject for the same offence to be twice put in jeopardy of life or limb; nor shall be compelled in any criminal case to be a witness against himself, nor be deprived of life, liberty, or property, without due process of law; nor shall private property be taken for public use, without just compensation.

Amendment VI

In all criminal prosecutions, the accused shall enjoy the right to a speedy and public trial, by an impartial jury of the State and district wherein the crime shall have been committed, which district shall have been previously ascertained by law, and to be informed of the nature and cause of the accusation; to be confronted with the witnesses against him; to have compulsory process for obtaining witnesses in his favor, and to have the Assistance of Counsel for his defence.

Amendment VII

In Suits at common law, where the value in controversy shall exceed twenty dollars, the right of trial by jury shall be preserved, and no fact tried by a jury, shall be otherwise re-examined in any Court of the United States, than according to the rules of the common law.

Amendment VIII

Excessive bail shall not be required, nor excessive fines imposed, nor cruel and unusual punishments inflicted.

Amendment IX

The enumeration in the Constitution, of certain rights, shall not be construed to deny or disparage others retained by the people.

Amendment X

The powers not delegated to the United States by the Constitution, nor prohibited by it to the States, are reserved to the States respectively, or to the people.

Amendments 11-27
The Constitution: Amendments 11-27

Constitutional Amendments 1-10 make up what is known as The Bill of Rights.
Amendments 11-27 are listed below.

AMENDMENT XI

Passed by Congress March 4, 1794. Ratified February 7, 1795.

Note: Article III, section 2, of the Constitution was modified by amendment 11.

The Judicial power of the United States shall not be construed to extend to any suit in law or equity, commenced or prosecuted against one of the United States by Citizens of another State, or by Citizens or Subjects of any Foreign State.

AMENDMENT XII
Passed by Congress December 9, 1803. Ratified June 15, 1804.

Note: A portion of Article II, section 1 of the Constitution was superseded by the 12th amendment.

The Electors shall meet in their respective states and vote by ballot for President and Vice-President, one of whom, at least, shall not be an inhabitant of the same state with themselves; they shall name in their ballots the person voted for as President, and in distinct ballots the person voted for as Vice-President, and they shall make distinct lists of all persons voted for as President, and of all persons voted for as Vice-President, and of the number of votes for each, which lists they shall sign and certify, and transmit sealed to the seat of the government of the United States, directed to the President of the Senate; -- the President of the Senate shall, in the presence of the Senate and House of Representatives, open all the certificates and the votes shall then be counted; -- The person having the greatest number of votes for President, shall be the President, if such number be a majority of the whole number of Electors appointed; and if no person have such majority, then from the persons having the highest numbers not exceeding three on the list of those voted for as President, the House of Representatives shall choose immediately, by ballot, the President. But in choosing the President, the votes shall be taken by states, the representation from each state having one vote; a quorum for this purpose shall consist of a member or members from two-thirds of the states, and a majority of all the states shall be necessary to a choice. [And if the House of Representatives shall not choose a President whenever the right of choice shall devolve upon them, before the fourth day of March next following, then the Vice-President shall act as President, as in case of the death or other constitutional disability of the President. --]* The person having the greatest number of votes as Vice-President, shall be the Vice-President, if such number be a majority of the whole number of Electors appointed, and if no person have a majority, then from the two highest numbers on the list, the Senate shall choose the Vice-President; a quorum for the purpose shall consist of two-thirds of the whole number of Senators, and a majority of the whole number shall be necessary to a choice. But no person constitutionally ineligible to the office of President shall be eligible to that of Vice-President of the United States.

*Superseded by section 3 of the 20th amendment.

AMENDMENT XIII
Passed by Congress January 31, 1865. Ratified December 6, 1865.

Note: A portion of Article IV, section 2, of the Constitution was superseded by the 13th amendment.

Section 1.
Neither slavery nor involuntary servitude, except as a punishment for crime whereof the party shall have been duly convicted, shall exist within the United States, or any place subject to their jurisdiction.

Section 2.
Congress shall have power to enforce this article by appropriate legislation.

AMENDMENT XIV
Passed by Congress June 13, 1866. Ratified July 9, 1868.

Note: Article I, section 2, of the Constitution was modified by section 2 of the 14th amendment.

Section 1.
All persons born or naturalized in the United States, and subject to the jurisdiction thereof, are citizens of the United States and of the State wherein they reside. No State shall make or enforce any law which shall abridge the privileges or immunities of citizens of the United States; nor shall any State deprive any person of life, liberty, or property, without due process of law; nor deny to any person within its jurisdiction the equal protection of the laws.

Section 2.
Representatives shall be apportioned among the several States according to their respective numbers, counting the whole number of persons in each State, excluding Indians not taxed. But when the right to vote at any election for the choice of electors for President and Vice-President of the United States, Representatives in Congress, the Executive and Judicial officers of a State, or the members of the Legislature thereof, is denied to any of the male inhabitants of such State, being twenty-one years of age,* and citizens of the United States, or in any way abridged, except for participation in rebellion, or other crime, the basis of representation therein shall be reduced in the proportion which the number of such male citizens shall bear to the whole number of male citizens twenty-one years of age in such State.

Section 3.
No person shall be a Senator or Representative in Congress, or elector of President and Vice-President, or hold any office, civil or military, under the United States, or under any State, who, having previously taken an oath, as a member of Congress, or as an officer of the United

States, or as a member of any State legislature, or as an executive or judicial officer of any State, to support the Constitution of the United States, shall have engaged in insurrection or rebellion against the same, or given aid or comfort to the enemies thereof. But Congress may by a vote of two-thirds of each House, remove such disability.

Section 4.
The validity of the public debt of the United States, authorized by law, including debts incurred for payment of pensions and bounties for services in suppressing insurrection or rebellion, shall not be questioned. But neither the United States nor any State shall assume or pay any debt or obligation incurred in aid of insurrection or rebellion against the United States, or any claim for the loss or emancipation of any slave; but all such debts, obligations and claims shall be held illegal and void.

Section 5.
The Congress shall have the power to enforce, by appropriate legislation, the provisions of this article.

*Changed by section 1 of the 26th amendment.

AMENDMENT XV
Passed by Congress February 26, 1869. Ratified February 3, 1870.

Section 1.
The right of citizens of the United States to vote shall not be denied or abridged by the United States or by any State on account of race, color, or previous condition of servitude--

Section 2.
The Congress shall have the power to enforce this article by appropriate legislation.

AMENDMENT XVI

Passed by Congress July 2, 1909. Ratified February 3, 1913.

Note: Article I, section 9, of the Constitution was modified by amendment 16.

The Congress shall have power to lay and collect taxes on incomes, from whatever source derived, without apportionment among the several States, and without regard to any census or enumeration.

AMENDMENT XVII

Passed by Congress May 13, 1912. Ratified April 8, 1913.

Note: Article I, section 3, of the Constitution was modified by the 17th amendment.

The Senate of the United States shall be composed of two Senators from each State, elected by the people thereof, for six years; and each Senator shall have one vote. The electors in each State shall have the qualifications requisite for electors of the most numerous branch of the State legislatures.

When vacancies happen in the representation of any State in the Senate, the executive authority of such State shall issue writs of election to fill such vacancies: Provided, That the legislature of any State may empower the executive thereof to make temporary appointments until the people fill the vacancies by election as the legislature may direct.

This amendment shall not be so construed as to affect the election or term of any Senator chosen before it becomes valid as part of the Constitution.

AMENDMENT XVIII

Passed by Congress December 18, 1917. Ratified January 16, 1919. Repealed by amendment 21.

Section 1.
After one year from the ratification of this article the manufacture, sale, or transportation of intoxicating liquors within, the importation thereof into, or the exportation thereof from the United States and all territory subject to the jurisdiction thereof for beverage purposes is hereby prohibited.

Section 2.
The Congress and the several States shall have concurrent power to enforce this article by appropriate legislation.

Section 3.
This article shall be inoperative unless it shall have been ratified as an amendment to the Constitution by the legislatures of the several States, as provided in the Constitution, within seven years from the date of the submission hereof to the States by the Congress.

AMENDMENT XIX

Passed by Congress June 4, 1919. Ratified August 18, 1920.

The right of citizens of the United States to vote shall not be denied or abridged by the United States or by any State on account of sex.

Congress shall have power to enforce this article by appropriate legislation.

AMENDMENT XX

Passed by Congress March 2, 1932. Ratified January 23, 1933.

Note: Article I, section 4, of the Constitution was modified by section 2 of this amendment. In addition, a portion of the 12th amendment was superseded by section 3.

Section 1.
The terms of the President and the Vice President shall end at noon on the 20th day of January, and the terms of Senators and Representatives at noon on the 3d day of January, of the years in which such terms would have ended if this article had not been ratified; and the terms of their successors shall then begin.

Section 2.
The Congress shall assemble at least once in every year, and such meeting shall begin at noon on the 3d day of January, unless they shall by law appoint a different day.

Section 3.
If, at the time fixed for the beginning of the term of the President, the President elect shall have died, the Vice President elect shall become President. If a President shall not have been chosen before the time fixed for the beginning of his term, or if the President elect shall have failed to qualify, then the Vice President elect shall act as President until a President shall have qualified; and the Congress may by law provide for the case wherein neither a President elect nor a Vice President elect shall have qualified, declaring who shall then act as President, or the manner in which one who is to act shall be selected, and such person shall act accordingly until a President or Vice President shall have qualified.

Section 4.
The Congress may by law provide for the case of the death of any of the persons from whom the House of Representatives may choose a President whenever the right of choice shall have devolved upon them, and for the case of the death of any of the persons from whom the

Senate may choose a Vice President whenever the right of choice shall have devolved upon them.

Section 5.
Sections 1 and 2 shall take effect on the 15th day of October following the ratification of this article.

Section 6.
This article shall be inoperative unless it shall have been ratified as an amendment to the Constitution by the legislatures of three-fourths of the several States within seven years from the date of its submission.

AMENDMENT XXI
Passed by Congress February 20, 1933. Ratified December 5, 1933.

Section 1.
The eighteenth article of amendment to the Constitution of the United States is hereby repealed.

Section 2.
The transportation or importation into any State, Territory, or possession of the United States for delivery or use therein of intoxicating liquors, in violation of the laws thereof, is hereby prohibited.

Section 3.
This article shall be inoperative unless it shall have been ratified as an amendment to the Constitution by conventions in the several States, as provided in the Constitution, within seven years from the date of the submission hereof to the States by the Congress.

AMENDMENT XXII
Passed by Congress March 21, 1947. Ratified February 27, 1951.

Section 1.

No person shall be elected to the office of the President more than twice, and no person who has held the office of President, or acted as President, for more than two years of a term to which some other person was elected President shall be elected to the office of the President more than once. But this Article shall not apply to any person holding the office of President when this Article was proposed by the Congress, and shall not prevent any person who may be holding the office of President, or acting as President, during the term within which this Article becomes operative from holding the office of President or acting as President during the remainder of such term.

Section 2.

This article shall be inoperative unless it shall have been ratified as an amendment to the Constitution by the legislatures of three-fourths of the several States within seven years from the date of its submission to the States by the Congress.

AMENDMENT XXIII
Passed by Congress June 16, 1960. Ratified March 29, 1961.

Section 1.
The District constituting the seat of Government of the United States shall appoint in such manner as the Congress may direct:

A number of electors of President and Vice President equal to the whole number of Senators and Representatives in Congress to which the District would be entitled if it were a State, but in no event more than the least populous State; they shall be in addition to those appointed by the States, but they shall be considered, for the purposes of the election of President and Vice President, to be electors appointed by a State; and they shall meet in the District and perform such duties as provided by the twelfth article of amendment.

Section 2.
The Congress shall have power to enforce this article by appropriate legislation.

AMENDMENT XXIV
Passed by Congress August 27, 1962. Ratified January 23, 1964.
Section 1.
The right of citizens of the United States to vote in any primary or other election for President or Vice President, for electors for President or Vice President, or for Senator or Representative in Congress, shall not be denied or abridged by the United States or any State by reason of failure to pay any poll tax or other tax.

Section 2.
The Congress shall have power to enforce this article by appropriate legislation.

AMENDMENT XXV
Passed by Congress July 6, 1965. Ratified February 10, 1967.

Note: Article II, section 1, of the Constitution was affected by the 25th amendment.

Section 1.
In case of the removal of the President from office or of his death or resignation, the Vice President shall become President.

Section 2.
Whenever there is a vacancy in the office of the Vice President, the President shall nominate a Vice President who shall take office upon confirmation by a majority vote of both Houses of Congress.

Section 3.

Whenever the President transmits to the President pro tempore of the Senate and the Speaker of the House of Representatives his written declaration that he is unable to discharge the powers and duties of his office, and until he transmits to them a written declaration to the contrary, such powers and duties shall be discharged by the Vice President as Acting President.

Section 4.

Whenever the Vice President and a majority of either the principal officers of the executive departments or of such other body as Congress may by law provide, transmit to the President pro tempore of the Senate and the Speaker of the House of Representatives their written declaration that the President is unable to discharge the powers and duties of his office, the Vice President shall immediately assume the powers and duties of the office as Acting President.

Thereafter, when the President transmits to the President pro tempore of the Senate and the Speaker of the House of Representatives his written declaration that no inability exists, he shall resume the powers and duties of his office unless the Vice President and a majority of either the principal officers of the executive department or of such other body as Congress may by law provide, transmit within four days to the President pro tempore of the Senate and the Speaker of the House of Representatives their written declaration that the President is unable to discharge the powers and duties of his office. Thereupon Congress shall decide the issue, assembling within forty-eight hours for that purpose if not in session. If the Congress, within twenty-one days after receipt of the latter written declaration, or, if Congress is not in session, within twenty-one days after Congress is required to assemble, determines by two-thirds vote of both Houses that the President is unable to discharge the powers and duties of his office, the Vice President shall continue to discharge the same as Acting President; otherwise, the President shall resume the powers and duties of his office.

AMENDMENT XXVI
Passed by Congress March 23, 1971. Ratified July 1, 1971.

Note: Amendment 14, section 2, of the Constitution was modified by section 1 of the 26th amendment.

Section 1.
The right of citizens of the United States, who are eighteen years of age or older, to vote shall not be denied or abridged by the United States or by any State on account of age.

Section 2.
The Congress shall have power to enforce this article by appropriate legislation.

AMENDMENT XXVII
Originally proposed Sept. 25, 1789. Ratified May 7, 1992.

No law, varying the compensation for the services of the Senators and Representatives, shall take effect, until an election of Representatives shall have intervened.

Chapter 12: The author's personal notes

Author David Lawrence of Dundalk (That's me.) Assembling this book made me feel as though I am a peer of every American from 1776 to 2016 and beyond.

Reading the words of the Declaration of Independence should and will inspire all Americans. Reading this document gives you the feeling of how much our founders wanted Liberty and Freedom from a ruler reaching to control them from a faraway distance shore across an ocean.

The grievances spelled out line after line show once started, they would never go back to a system that gave all supreme power to a Monarch.

They wanted and knew that Laws had to be enacted that would benefit citizens living in the colonies that were reasonable and fitting for their time and place.

When reading the Constitution of the United States and the 27 Amendments to the document, you come away with a sense of how Head Strong we were when starting this new Republic.

It was pure, it was simple and it was honest. All citizens counted and mattered, there was to be no higher or lower class in this New Republic, in this New Democracy that we had just invented.

The Declaration of Independence refers to our creator, " That all are created equal, that they are endowed by their Creator with certain unalienable rights, among these are Life, Liberty and the Pursuit of Happiness."

Nowhere, while reading there documents, did even the slightest suggestion, that our form of Government would endeavor to try to control citizens' daily life and activities as the King of England attempted to try from distance far shores.

Our Early Representatives could not have ever conceived our New National Government becoming the country's largest employer and having to go into so much world debt to sustain this massive growth.

Our country and our whole nation, state by state, need to get back on track, The Government of the United States was formed to protect citizens and property of citizens, and to keep safe our laws as written in the Constitution.

Our new Constitution gave all power to the citizens of our new democracy with the President as steward of our causes. The Constitution gave the several states the responsibility of passing local laws that affected their own boundaries and not to interfere with other States or the National Government.

The National Government was formed to regulate, not intimidate States Rights, after all, the citizens of Georgia and the citizens of Vermont have vast differences in everyday life experiences and our Government at the very beginning knew (one size does not fit all).

Reading from the last 8 years of Executive Orders, it becomes quite clear that the President is infringing into ordinary citizens Life, Liberty and Pursuit of Happiness by intruding into everyday life with the President's Executive Orders.

As King George of England so openly said "I know more about what's good for my subjects then they do " and I will force them to comply with my decrees to prove the King is always right.

After all, my subjects must be cared for like children, with a strong hand and kept in line, so they think they are happy.

Summing it up, our two Houses should pass all laws together that effect Life, Liberty and the Pursuit of Happiness. They should empower each State Government with applying laws that directly benefit their citizens.

California, Texas, Michigan and Maryland all have different climates and the means to support their citizens' individual needs.

When California voters chose to support the LGBT community and voters from a different State chose not to do so, it should, under the United States Constitution, be right and just for the States to vote without interference from the Federal Government.

Having said all this, the President of the United States should return to the role that was envisioned he would preside over. Stewardship of a great nation, the United States of America.

Amen

Chapter 13: A Scary Non-Fiction

After the President signs an Executive Order, the White House sends it to the Office of the Federal Register where upon it is numbered consecutively as part of a series and Published in the daily Federal Register shortly after received.

DID YOU GET YOUR COPY YET?

Don't let it bother anyone that all 247 Executive Orders from the President's term of eight years start with the lucky or unlucky number thirteen.

Do the citizens of the United States even know when a new Executive Order Law signed by the President goes into effect?

Don't let it bother our military or veterans that a total of five revisions were made to the Manual of Courts Martial during the President's two terms in office for a very hard to read 173 Pages of Executive Orders.

Don't let it bother you that at least over 40 Executive Orders were written and signed by the President to establish various committees, advisory boards, and councils, all appointed by the President. (Good way to pay off campaign workers or individual donors?)

EO 13731 of 24 June 2016 Global Entrepreneurship: (Quote from the Order). "It is in the National interest for the Federal Government to support Global entrepreneurship and the American private sector linking capital, new networks and markets." Providing skills and backing up out of the country jobs. (That's scary.)

EO 13732 of 01 July 2016 Policy on Pre and Post Strike measures to address civilian casualties in U.S. operations.

Para (b) (ii) gets to the message of this Executive Order - Acknowledge U.S. Responsibility for civilian casualties and offer payment to civilians or family members.

Please ask any veteran back from the Middle East conflicts how you can tell a civilian from a combat troop?

EO 13725 of 15 April 2016. Steps to increase competition using Government agencies to compile lists of companies that need more regulation according to the Federal Government guidelines.

EO 13718 of 09 February 2016:   Commission on Enhancing National Cybersecurity:
How is that working out big fellow?

EO 13715 of 18 December 2015:   Adjustments of certain rates of pay:

This one seems to pop up the end or first of the year...Good Old Boys getting Perks from the President. Don't know, does the general public know?

EO 13708 of 30 September 2015: Continuance or reestablishment of Federal Advisory Committees.
Just what we need, more easy jobs for Presidential Appointees.

How do WE get on these committees?

EO 13707 of 15 September 2015: Using Behavioral Science Insights to better serve the American People...

A committee to judge how families, communities, and businesses respond to the President's Rules and Regulations.

EO 13705 of 03 September 2015: Designating the International Renewable Agency as a Public International Organization ENTITLED to enjoy certain Privileges, Exemptions, and Immunities.
That says it all. I can't add to that.

EO 13688 of 16 January 2015: Federal support for local law enforcement equipment acquisition.

Yes local law enforcement you may have excess equipment, but first you have to jump through many hoops, including recommendation from many government agencies and you have to understand this Executive Order first...lots of luck...

EO 13673 of 31 July 2014: Fair Pay and Safe Workplaces:

The President must stay up all night just trying to get into Americans' daily life!

EO 13665 of 08 April 2014:   Non-Retaliation for Disclosure of Compensation Information:
Hey Government Workers! You can ask all you want about anyone's wage to see if they are making more money than you without Fear of Adverse Action against you.
This keeps everyone happy and content with his or her paycheck!

EO 13659 of 19 February 2014:   Streamlining the Export/Import Process for America's Businesses: We must improve Trade environment through the development of innovative policies and operational processes that promote effective application of regulatory controls. (He just cannot stop his pen from jumping into everything, can he?)

EO 13653:   of 01 November 2013:   Preparing the United States for the impacts of Climate Change of 01 November 2013:   Section 7: (A) Establishment: To inform Federal efforts to support climate preparedness and resilience, there is established a State, Local and Tribal Leaders Task Force on Climate Preparedness and Resilience. Great...CALL OUT THE MEDICINE MAN AND HAVE A RAIN DANCE!

EO 13647 of 26 June 2013: Establishing the White House Council on Native American Affairs:
Why after over a hundred years is the Native Americans not United States citizens and are still recognized as a separate country inside American Borders? Makes no sense. We don't need reservations in the 21st Century. (Go Washington Redskins)

EO 13646 of 25 June 2013: Establishing the President's Advisory Council on Financial Capability for Young Americans:

(B) (Iii). Effectively assess the financial capability, including both financial knowledge and Financial behaviors of Young Americans.

(Use late night shows to conduct interviews on the streets) Lots of luck with that!

EO 13623 of 10 August 2012: Preventing and Responding to Violence Against Women and Girls Globally:
Recognizing that Gender Based violence undermines not only the safety, dignity and Human Rights of the millions of individuals who experience it, but also the public health, economic stability and security of Nations, it is the policy and practice of the Executive

Branch of the United States Government to have a multi-year strategy that will more effectively prevent and respond to gender based violence GLOBALLY.

(WOW!) The president really wants to run the world...watch out, Sir. In the year 2016, the Brits will hand you your hat over your BREXIT speech in England....

EO 13617 of 25 June 2012: Blocking property of the Russian Federation relating to the disposition of highly enriched uranium extracted from Nuclear Weapons.
(That's cool, now how about Iran?)

EO 13610 of 10 May 2012: Identifying and Reducing Regulatory Burdens.
STILL WAITING!

EO 13609 of 01 May 2012: Promoting International Regulatory Cooperation
(We hope that works out better than National Cooperation!)

EO 13608 of 01 May 2012: Prohibiting Certain Transactions with and Suspending Entry into the United States of Foreign Sanctions Evaders with respect to Iran and Syria

It's been four years, Mr. President, had any luck with that YET?

EO 13599 of 05 February 2012:   Blocking Property of the Government of Iran and Iranian Financial Institutions
(Gave it all back, what a waste of time.)

EO 13595 of 19 December 2011: Instituting a National Action Plan on Women, Peace, and Security:
SAY WHAT! Does that even sound like it could happen?

EO 13589 of 09 November 2011:   PROMOTING EFFICIENT SPENDING
(Good Job, but Check our National Debt in the year 2016...)

EO 13587 of 07 October 2011: Structural Reforms to Improve the Security of Classified Network and the Responsible Sharing and Safeguarding of Classified Information

(State Department must have missed this one; could you please resend it ASAP?)

EO 13583 of 18 August 2011:   Establishing A coordinated Government Wide Initiative to Promote Diversity and Inclusion in the Federal Work Force

(How much Diversity and Inclusion are we talking about?)

EO 13581 of 24 July 2011:   Blocking Property of Transnational Criminal Organizations
(Are they talking about Transnational Dressers or just Criminals?)

EO 13579 of 11 July 2011:   Regulation and Independent Regulatory Agencies
WOW...This is when it started and it just got bigger and better over the next five years!

EO 13578 of 06 July 2011: Coordinating Policies on Automotive Communities and Workers
Ever wonder what happen to the Auto Industry in America?

EO 13577 of 15 June 2011:   Establishment of the SELECT USA Initiative
Sounds like the President is inviting Foreign Nationals to enter the United States to be more Competitive Global...

EO 13576 of 13 June 2011: Delivering an Efficient and Accountable Government
Did the IRS and State Departments get this Order?

EO 13571 of 27 April 2011:   Streamlining Service Delivery and Improving Customer Service
    Same Question as above Order 13576.

EO 13564 of 31 January 2011: Establishment of the President's Council on Jobs and Competitiveness
Create jobs, opportunity, and Prosperity for the American people by ensuring the availability of non-partisan advice to the President from participants in and experts on the Economy:
Must have been great advice...look at our jobs mess.

EO 13562 of 27 December 2010: Recruiting and Hiring Students and Recent Graduates:
Sounds like a Recruitment for flipping Hamburgers

EO 13560 of 14 December 2010: White House Council for Community Solutions:
FINALLY, a job he's qualified for...

EO 13556 of 04 November 2010: Controlled Unclassified Information.

AGAIN...does STATE read any of these Executive Orders?

EO 13552 of 31 August 2010: (NO TITLE AVAILABLE).

FINALLY...one we can all understand...

EO 13547 of 19 July 2010: Stewardship of the Ocean, our Coasts, and the Great Lakes

OK. Listen up; you fish will comply with my orders...

EO 13537 of 14 April 2010: Interagency Group on Insular Areas.

Watch out...Big Brother is coming....

EO 13526 of 29 December 2010: Classified National Security Information.
Not even going to touch this one...its 27 pages long. Lots of luck!

EO 13520 of 20 November 2009: Reducing Improper Payments.

Five Pages long to tell employees not to steal. Big Brother IS WATCHING...

EO 13492. Of 22 January 2009: Review and Disposition of Individuals Detained at the Guantanamo Bay Naval Base and Closure of Detention Facilities.

"Promptly to Close detention facilities"

Well it has been eight years that have passed and closing is not as easy as promised, maybe in the next 8 years it will get done. In the meantime, keep killing them on the battlefield instead of locking them up in safe, well-maintained holding cells.